CONVERSATIONS ON GROWING OLDER

CONVERSATIONS ON GROWING OLDER

by

Cornelis Gilhuis

translated by

Cor W. Barendrecht

William B. Eerdmans Publishing Company

Translated by Cor W. Barendrecht from the Dutch,
Hoe dichter ik nader.
Published by arrangement with Zomer & Keuning,
Wageningen, The Netherlands.

Chapter 6 appeared in slightly different form in *The Banner,*
November 1, 1974, © CRC Board of Publications, 1974.

Library of Congress Cataloging in Publication Data:

Gilhuis, C.
    Conversations on growing older.

    Translation of Hoe dichter ik nader.
    1. Aged — Religious life.   2. Death.   3. Future life.
I. Title.
BV4580.G5413   248'.85   77-1504
ISBN 0-8028-1694-0

As I draw nearer
        to the house of my Father,
I yearn more and more
        for the heavenly mansion,
Where after life's battle
        my King's blessing awaits.

What hinders me yet?
        I shall go to God's children.
I hear now the glad sounds
        of heavenly servants,
Who jubilantly call me
        to my Father's house.
— *Hiëronymous van Alphen, 1803*

Acknowledgments

The Bible text used in this book is the Revised Standard Version Bible, copyright 1946, 1952, and © 1971 by the Division of Christian Education of the National Council of Churches of Christ in the United States of America.

For the use of hymns and psalms in the English edition, I wish to acknowledge the following works: The Hymnal of the Protestant Episcopal Church in the United States of America, 1952 edition; The Book of Praise: Anglo-Genevan Psalter, first complete edition, 1912; The Psalter Hymnal of the Christian Reformed Church, 1959 edition.

Grateful acknowledgment is made to Marie J. Post for permission to use her poem "Awake at Night," quoted on page 49. Poetry by R. Houwink (p. 51), Helen Swarth (pp. 57, 58), Archilles Mussche (p. 134), and Guido Gezelle (p. 174) has been translated liberally and not necessarily poetically.

Special thanks is due Marten H. Woudstra of Calvin Theological Seminary for his advice in solving some difficulties in interpreting the Psalms.

Contents

IN THE DOOR

BEHIND THE DOOR

Getting Acquainted

In this book I imagine myself sitting down to talk with you, my brothers and sisters in the faith, who with me "love the appearing of our Lord Jesus," as Paul says to Timothy (2 Timothy 4:8). I hope that this book will also come into the hands of many people who do not yet know this Savior. Maybe they will come to believe. May God grant that they do.

I do not know you, of course. But I know one thing about you: you are no longer young. The evening of your life has come and you are nearing the end. This has brought about many changes in your life. An elderly person is at a different point in life from a younger one. In my pastoral work I have seen and heard much of the great change. I think I know something of the difficulties, questions, and expectations you face.

I should like it if we could do some talking together. As an older person, you usually value a good talk. Getting older means getting lonesome. Therefore, a visit is welcome. We won't make our talks too long or too deep. You are not so much interested in that kind of talk anymore. You would rather talk about what needs to be said, what is essential, the things that really matter.

First we shall talk about life just *before* the door to eternity. Then we shall say something about being *in* that door: dying. And last, we shall have something to say about life *behind* that door. The publisher has used a larger size of type than usual to make it a little easier for you to read.

C. G.

BEFORE THE DOOR

1. Alone

For many elderly people life *before* the door to eternity is a lonely life. When I envision myself sitting next to you, I see you sitting in your chair near the window, or on the bed . . . alone. I don't know many elderly people who are still caught up in the busy, bustling stream of human life; certainly not when they are past seventy.

"I'm alone so much . . . , they have forgotten me . . . , I don't count any longer." I have heard you say this more than once.

Yes, you sit in silence so much that the lively noise at a party or at a family gathering actually is a little too much for you. You're not used to noise anymore.

Yet, this silence sometimes can become an obsession, even if only a brief one. At such a time you may wish: if only someone would come in and talk with me quietly. If only so-and-so, my husband or wife, my employer, or my friend, would come to see me. But they are no longer here.

This getting to be more and more alone may have begun when you retired. You came to stand alongside of a busy, everyday life. You became like someone watching heavy traffic from the side of the road, without being a part of the stream. At first your colleagues came to see you once in a while, but then they came less frequently. Younger people took your place at work, people who didn't know you.

Or you used to be active as a homemaker or as a housewife. Everything in the family revolved around you. Now, you hear the doorbell and people's voices from a distance. It doesn't affect you anymore. Other people now have taken over and go about things their own way, without you. You can't keep up with it as well as you used to. You just sit there, or lie there — perhaps even in a rest home among people who didn't know you before. You sit there, alone.

Along with this social loneliness came loneliness in the circle of family and friends. One after the other fell away into death. The number of contemporaries with whom you associate has become smaller and smaller. A lot of obituaries have passed through your hands in these past years.

One by one you've had to lose your husband or wife, your brother, your sister.

You are still here. Alone.

True, the children and grandchildren are still here, but they have their own preoccupations, in which you feel an outsider. Even if they haven't forgotten you, they still don't have much time for you. And if you have never been married, you even miss that relationship.

For many elderly persons a loneliness related to the church has been added. You used to go to church with God's people. Looking back, you appreciate this even more now than you did then. How many fine Sundays were among these! Now this is no longer possible. When others go to church, you are sitting at home — alone.

Of course, a radio service is fine. And the minister's visit, if he has time — and does not forget you. But these are substitutes. They do not compare with what you used to enjoy, experience, and receive in this respect. . . .

Maybe your loneliness is even more severe because you have become deaf. How sad this is. You can see people talk, laugh, gesticulate, but you don't hear a word of what they say. You cannot follow them. Even while you are in lively company, you are alone.

I have known a few elderly persons who, besides being deaf, also turned blind. Then you're among people almost like a plant, which has its place in the room but cannot see or hear anything. Fortunately, this does not occur too frequently.

But growing old does more or less mean getting lonesome.

More than one elderly person will see himself in the complaint: "I am most distressed and lonely; Waves of trouble over me roll."

What shall I say about these things?

First, let me point out to you the dangers here. The first danger — yes, a sin — is that of becoming bitter because of these experiences. Your face gets a forbidding expression, and your voice takes on an accusing tone. Understandable though this attitude may be, your loneliness will tend to get worse because of it. You will turn away the people who still do come to visit you. They will come less and less, and soon not at all. "You have to listen to so many complaints there," they will say. Of course, this is not the right attitude for them to take, but it is certainly understandable. Perhaps you would do the same thing.

The second danger is that when you get lonesome everything so easily may come to revolve around you.

15

You are preoccupied with yourself. You unlearn what once came almost naturally: considering other persons and thinking of their need. If we are left to ourselves, our self-centeredness so easily grows worse.

"A friend is one who shows me my mistakes," the proverb goes. May I as a friend warn you against an egocentric, self-seeking attitude towards life? In the loneliness of getting older such an attitude towards life finds fertile ground. By all means continue to show an interest in your fellow humans and in your environment. When visitors come, don't talk exclusively about yourself, your past, your problems. Inquire about the life and work of those who come to visit you. In these circumstances too the saying applies: "Whoever loses his life . . . will save it" (Luke 9:24). Such an old brother or sister one still likes to visit. Such a one is not easily forgotten. The one who gives always receives in return.

It is, in my opinion, to a large extent in your own hand to prevent your loneliness from growing still greater than it has.

And then — a Christian really is never alone. He says with the Psalm writer, "For my father and mother have forsaken me, but the Lord will take me up" (Psalm 27:10).

The Lord is continuously with you. He always holds your hand. How beautifully God says this to you through the mouth of Isaiah: "Even to your old age I am He, and to grey hairs I will carry you. I have made, and I will bear; I will carry and will save" (Isaiah 46:4). Does not comfort flow from all sides of this beautiful verse? I think, too, of what Christ himself said: "I am with you always, to the close of the age" (Matthew 28:20).

Always. Even in the days when you have grown old and lonesome.

Dear brothers and sisters, don't ever forget that. Jesus is invisibly with you, *always*. "I *am*," it says; not "I will be with you some day" or "Once I was with you." No, "Every day I *am* with you." He greets you every morning. How seldom we live in and by that certainty! Do not live, then, as poorly as the unbeliever does when he grows old.

You always have a distinguished guest. Set the Lord always before you. Sing with W. C. Dix:

> Alleluia! He is near us,
>   Faith believes, nor questions how:
> Though the cloud from sight received Him,
>   When the forty days were o'er,
> Shall our hearts forget His promise,
>   "I am with you evermore"?

Finally, there is also a communion of the saints, even if we do not see them.

"When you pray," Jesus said, "go into your room and close the door" (Matthew 6:6). He refers one who prays to a place of loneliness. But in the same breath he says, "Pray then like this: *Our* Father." In that loneliness I must, therefore, think of these other children of God. Though I don't see them, I must have communion with them. As in a mother's thinking her children are always around her, even when they are far away, so it is also with the believer. He knows himself always belonging to the great community of God's people.

No, the more I think about it, the less I believe that an old Christian really is lonesome and alone.

And you will, after all, certainly agree with that.

2. No More

It was his eighty-fifth birthday. What a ripe old age! During the years of his life two world wars had been fought.

Now we were sitting down together, and he suddenly said, "Above my life I could now write the words: 'no more.' "

My wife is . . . no more.

My friends are . . . no more.

My freedom is . . . no more. I sit here in a home for the aged.

My house I have . . . no more.

My good health . . . no more.

My good hearing . . . no more.

My walking so easily . . . no more.

My memory as accurate . . . no more.

All: no more, no more, pastor.

Every aged person can make his own list of "no more's."

One may have a somewhat longer list than another,

but everyone has one. And the older you are, the longer the list grows.

Finally, to each list the entry will be added: He or she is ... no more. ...

I take my pocket Bible then (and I do so now with you), and I say: Do you know that the Bible also said that in a poetic way, long ago?

We read then, with some added explanations, Ecclesiastes 12; and we'll do the same now.

Remember also your Creator in the days of your youth, before the evil days come, and the years draw nigh, when you will say, "I have no pleasure in them."

"*The evil days,*" that is the day of old age, the time of deterioration, of the "no more."

"*When you will say, 'I have no pleasure in them,'*" yes, that is still the case today: all of us like to grow old, but no one likes to be old.

"*Remember also your Creator in the days of your youth*": how shall we grow old well if we haven't found the Creator in our youth? A good old age is prepared for in one's youth. Why not tell that to the young people who come to visit you?

"*Before the sun and the light and the moon and the stars are darkened and the clouds return after the rain*"; here old age is compared to a cloudy, dark landscape, whipped by one rainstorm after another.

"*In the day when the keepers of the house tremble.*" These keepers are the hands. What an inconvenience they cause when they begin to tremble, so that you spill food when you eat and drink. No one understands how embarrassed you may feel in company of other people. You have lost your steadiness and sureness.

19

"And the strong men are bent"; these are the legs. Just a moment ago, an old man passed my window, small step by small step; his legs are bent. . . . The springiness has left them.

"And the grinders cease because they are few." This refers to the front teeth and the molars. Modern times have found in dentures a beautiful substitute for this shortcoming of old age, but I know some older people who do not have them. One person I know has a single tooth in the upper jaw; but as a loner that tooth can no longer serve its purpose.

"And those that look through the windows are dimmed." The eyes lack luster; they don't see very well anymore. Even glasses or a magnifying glass does not always suffice.

"And the doors on the street are shut." The ears no longer take in all the sounds.

"When the sound of the grinding is low, and one rises up at the voice of a bird." The mouth is compared to a mill. From a mill comes sound. In man, this sound is the voice. But that voice becomes weaker, thinner; the sound less rich and resonant.

"They are afraid also of what is high." How difficult climbing the stairway gets to be when you have grown old. Sometimes people move to a main floor apartment for that reason. And the aged no longer go hiking in the mountains.

"And terrors are in the way." Yes, when a small boy on a bicycle approaches you on the sidewalk, you suddenly stop, afraid and uncertain. And crossing the street in a busy city. . . .

"The almond tree blossoms." One's hair turns grey or white, like the blossom of the almond tree just before dropping off.

"The grasshopper drags itself along." The grass-

hoppers refer to the joints, which are no longer as flexible; bending and kneeling are difficult.

"And desire fails." Today, perhaps, we would say: when vitamin preparations no longer help, and nothing can stimulate the appetite for food and for life.

"Because man goes to his eternal home, and the mourners go about the streets." Everything ends in death, in the eternal destiny of man.

"Before the silver cord is snapped, or the golden bowl is broken, or the pitcher is broken at the fountain." Here death is described by two beautiful images: a lamp that falls and breaks, and a pitcher that shatters into fragments at the well. Life is precious; therefore the passage speaks of the *silver* cord and the *golden* bowl or lamp.

"And the dust returns to the earth as it was, and the spirit returns to God who gave it." Without any figure of speech the end is now described.

American psychologist Stanley Hall once called Ecclesiastes 12 the most pessimistic description of old age ever written. How much different are the popular books about old age. "Keep smiling," they say. "Life *begins* at forty."

But which is more honest: the Bible, or this type of writing? Doesn't all that is of the earth end in that "no more?" This the writer of Ecclesiastes presents to you with honesty. In this matter, too, the Bible is trustworthy.

Yet, the writer of Ecclesiastes is not quite as pessimistic as Stanley Hall takes him to be. For above this "no more," the writer sees glimmering the promise of the living God, who does not forsake the work of his hands. God is also present in the day of adversity (see chapter 7:14). He watches from heaven and he keeps his promise. And even though the writer of Ecclesiastes depicts these things in somewhat of a twilight, in the New Testament the full light rises like the sun over the "no more." So we should not read Ecclesiastes 12 without also reading 2 Corinthians 4:16, and what follows.

In that passage Paul, too, speaks of that "no more," when he says, *"Though our outer nature is wasting away"* — in other words, even though we visibly deteriorate.

But Paul immediately adds, *"We do not lose heart."* Why doesn't this believer lose heart? Because he knows, *"our inner* — human — *nature is being renewed every day,"* and because with all believers he does not *"look to the things that are seen; for the things that are seen are transient* — they pass away — *but the things that are unseen are eternal."*

The inner man . . . by that is meant the life the believer has with his Savior. The older one gets, the nearer to him one draws. The greater the breakdown of the temporal is, the more the ties are strengthened with him, the Eternal One. Though flesh and heart may fail, God is your rock, your share eternally.

What is the condition of your inner life? Nothing remains, if that inner life is not present. What do you look for — the invisible or the visible? Are you, in spite of these "no more's," of good courage? It is possible, through Christ who strengthens us!

3. *Not Yet*

It has been said that young people can write above their lives, "not yet" — the opposite of the title of our previous talk.

You may hear younger people say: I haven't finished school yet; I'm not yet engaged; not married yet; not yet settled in a profession. Then they may get a little older and still say, We don't have any children yet, or the children haven't found their place in life as yet, we haven't reached the peak of our earnings yet, we haven't reached our retirement age yet.

Little by little the "not yet" of the younger ones turns into the "no more" of the older persons.

Young people say "not yet" because the future and the road of life still lies ahead of them. They still must make history. Youth and the future, it often is said, belong together.

You, on the contrary, have your life behind you; you already have made history; you have walked the larger part of the road of life. You are looking back.

You begin to live in the past. One could say, too, that old age and the past belong together.

And yet . . . is this so?

If *this* life means everything to you, it is true. How movingly this has been described in a novel I once read entitled *The Great Hall,* by Jacoba Van Velde. It is by no means a Christian book. On the contrary. But I can recommend it nonetheless. I have seldom been so impressed as I was when reading this book with the poverty of growing older and dying without Jesus Christ. It brought tears to my eyes.

The old woman whose life is described in this book must, like every old person, let go of everything little by little. When she has landed in a home for the aged, she has only one view: the great hall. The great hall is the place where one ends up when he becomes ill and is going to die. Everyone in the home knows this, and so all of them view this hall with a certain anxiety. The woman says the great hall is the only thing that still awaits her.

How terrible! And then to think that a judgment also follows. You would be inclined to turn around to avoid taking another look into the future if this were all.

But how richly faith in Jesus Christ can shine through at this point. That faith also has a view on a large hall in one's old age. But it is quite a different view from the one in the home for the aged described above. It is a happy hall, for which a child of God can yearn strongly in his best moments.

A Christian does not have the most important events behind him; these are still coming. Having grown old, he has life behind him, but Life (with a capital L) is still coming.

He does not say, "I have nothing left to expect,"

because he still has tremendous things to expect and experience. "My desire is to be with Christ, for that is far better," says Paul (Philippians 1:23). "How long it takes. Why hasn't Jesus come to get me yet?" many a dying Christian has asked me.

A Christian, too, in his old age can write above his life: "not yet." In this respect he has remained young. The future and the old Christian really belong together. Because,

> As I draw nearer
> to the house of my Father,
> I yearn more and more
> for the heavenly mansion,
> where after life's battle
> my King's blessing awaits.

I read somewhere of two "gentlemen" who were standing at a bus stop with an old lady. Loudly enough for her to hear, one of them said, referring to her, "She has seen her better days."

"I beg your pardon," the lady said, "I believe I may call myself a Christian, and so, for me, the best is yet to come!"

And when a Russian bishop was put in front of a firing squad, he called out, "Come on, you dead ones, fire! I am going to *live!*"

The best is yet to come. The Christian is going to live, even though he may have died. Therefore the Bible can say that the righteous shall remain green and fresh in old age, that they renew their youth like an eagle. In a real sense, believing people, people who know God, actually never grow old, because as long as they are here, they reach out for the future. They say, just like young people, "not yet!"

Do you say this too? Can you sing:

> As for me, I shall behold thy face
>   in righteousness;
> when I awake, I shall be satisfied
>   with beholding thy form (Psalm 17:15)?

4. Sacred Dissatisfaction

There are older people whom I particularly like to sit next to. They still seem so happy. They complain little and give the clear impression that they have much to be thankful for.

"We still have it so good, Pastor," they say. "People take good care of us and make things easy for us."

When you walk into their room — perhaps chilly or wet from the rain — and see them sitting there cozily in front of the fireplace, you can understand that very well. You understand too when they add, "I hope the Lord will spare my life."

Yet, sometimes I wonder — I will say this honestly — shouldn't they long much more for eternal glory? When they sing and speak joyfully about the present are they really able also to sing with the Psalmist: "Thy steadfast love is better than life" (Psalm 63:3)?

I also have heard the opposite reaction. "I hope the Lord will take me away," I hear, especially when the difficulties of growing older become so great that one would rather say farewell to this life.

I say this is the opposite, but actually it is the same. Just think. In the first case one doesn't want to go as yet, because life is still so good (cozy room, good bed, delicious cup of coffee, good rest, good care); in the other case one is quite willing to go, because life has become so difficult. In both cases "the good life now" dominates. In both cases life now is found actually to be better than the life that awaits in glory.

Of course, I may yet long to stay here for a while if my staying is useful for God's dominion. It was the apostle Paul's opinion that it was better for God's children if he could stay alive. But if, as in your case, the task has for the most part been completed, should not the pull toward God, toward serving him perfectly without sin, become increasingly stronger?

Is it good if this longing does not grow within you? You aren't like the drowning person who, as he sinks deeper, grasps tighter onto a broken reed to save his life, are you? Too many aged persons are like that. The more life breaks down, the more they tighten their clasp around this life: their pipe of tobacco, their cup of coffee, becomes everything to them.

But a Christian will likely begin to think more and more of the life in glory that awaits. I wish I could discover, among the many older Christians with whom I speak, more of that kind of longing for heaven — not as an *escape* from this life but as an *entrance* into glory that can't even be compared with the present.

We are not Christians in *name only,* are we? A non-Christian doctor recently said to me, "I don't believe there are any real Christians, because none of them want to die." If by that he meant that he seldom noticed anything of "the desire to depart and be with Christ" (Philippians 1:23), this certainly puts us to shame! A woman whose husband had fallen asleep in Jesus shortly after he was retired complained to me, "But he has only been able to enjoy his pension for such a short time!" Doesn't that sound a little strange, coming from someone who is called a Christian? Would I regret the loss of a dime if this brought me a million dollars? Does anything compare to the glory that shall be revealed unto us?

If in the Christian life the service of God is the highest ideal, shouldn't we then desire to serve God in perfection at his side — particularly when we stand so close to the door to eternity?

A sacred dissatisfaction must overpower us. We, too, says Paul, "groan inwardly as we wait for adoption as sons, the redemption of our bodies" (Romans 8:23).

Groaning, sighing, yearning, stretching out toward it: *sacred dissatisfaction* is the meaning of Paul's words.

"Yes, *but*," you say, "if only I could know for sure. . . ."

To that I have nothing to say right now, except, "Are you not certain of that as yet? Do you let Jesus stand knocking, before the door of your heart? Do you trust him yet?"

Remember the Psalmist's words: "He has not rejected my prayer, or removed his steadfast love" (Psalm 66:20).

5. How Time Flies!

How often do you say, "How time flies!"? The older one gets, the faster the weeks and years fly by. *Seem* to fly by, that is, because the clock in your room of course ticks at the same rate of speed as when you crawled on the floor as an infant.

When you were young, time often did not go fast enough for you. Young people don't say, "How time flies!" nearly as often as older persons do. This has several reasons. In particular it is because young people expect so much. They stretch out to reach all kinds of things. If they were only finished at school. . . . If they were only married. . . . If only. . . .

Life still offers scores of possibilities. Young people live in expectation, and waiting always lasts long. To them, the hands of the clock move very slowly.

But what may people who have grown old still expect from this life? They are quite happy when everything remains as it was. The little life that is left and the years shrink visibly. And so they say, "How time flies!"

Here, too, everything becomes different when we do not only set our hopes on the things of this life — the things that are seen — but look forward to "the city which has foundations, whose builder and maker is God" (Hebrews 11:10). Then even at an advanced age time does not go quite fast enough.

"It takes so long before the Savior comes." "I am yearning to see God in glory," I hear some witness. Then in the heart the poet's words resound:

> Lord Jesus, why do you tarry still longer,
> every hour our yearning grows deeper and stronger.

And this longing person may jubilantly say:

> When shall that hour have come
> When my rejoicing soul its own free power
> May use in going home!
> — *J. M. Meyfart, 1626*

Or:

> When thou dost bid us come,
> Then open wide the gates of pearl
> And call thy servants home.
> — *Godfrey Thring, 1886*

How is it for you: does time go quickly or sluggishly?

6. The Refresher Course

"And, how do you like it?" I asked a man who had retired just the other day.

"Fine, Pastor, very fine," was the answer. "I have my newspaper, my books. Every morning I take a brisk walk. I can help my wife a little with her work. I run errands for her. I peel the potatoes, and I even help her vacuum. I like it very much. The Lord makes the evening of my life beautiful. And then, I can still do something for the church...."

"Yes," his wife seconds. "I discover talents in him I had never imagined he possessed. We have a good life together. These days I am having my tea brought to me in bed. Before, he hardly knew where to find the teapot!"

When I saw them sitting at the fireplace, cozy and warm, I thought: "It really isn't so bad to be old and retired. I'll give up the ideal I had as a young man: to die with my boots on. I would like to experience this!"

I also asked another.

"Do you enjoy your retirement?"

He looked at me with an ironic expression on his face. "You did say, 'retired,' didn't you? Well, I still don't know what that word means. Or perhaps it means this, that I'm even busier than before. Yes, you are fortunate to catch me home. This is an exception, you see. Busy, busy, and busy some more! President of this, secretary of that.... I supplement my income with all kinds of temporary jobs. Social security doesn't make you rich, you know. No, life is at least as hurried as always."

"I am seeing my husband even less than before," his wife sighs wearily. "I would like to see things differently...."

"Dad ought to know better," says the adult daughter who still lives with them. "It isn't necessary; half as much as he does would do just as well."

When I heard this man talking busily and acting important and then noticed these faces of disapproval next to him, I thought: "No, this is not the way to do it. I wouldn't like to be retired that way. Something is wrong here."

I asked the same question of a third person.

"Pastor, don't mention it," he said, "it's a *horror!* I can't stand it any longer. Pardon my saying so, but I'm bored stiff. I don't like reading. Never have been a reader. And my wife's cackling around me simply irritates me! What else am I to do? I can't walk the streets or play babysitter for the grandchildren all day, can I?"

"Often he is intolerable," his wife said with a look of reproach. "I wish his employer would call him back immediately."

"So do I," he answered. "The sooner the better."

Then, too, I knew: I would not like to spend my last years this way.

Again I asked someone. And you can ask many people the same question. These days thousands of people are retired. Nearly everyone lives past the age of retirement. If you think of the population of the world as a pyramid, the tip is becoming wider, as the death rate drops, while the base (determined by youth) becomes smaller and smaller as the birth rate declines.

But back to my conversation.

The man I asked the question of got up and walked to the cupboard.

"It isn't easy, Pastor," I heard him say as he laid down a medal in front of me. "Look, I received this for forty years of faithful service. Never missed a day. Always worked with pleasure — with heart and soul, so to speak. And now, here I am. Pushed aside. You just don't count anymore. Life goes on without you as if you've never been there.

"I must admit to you honestly, that at first I would drive in the direction of the office in the morning. Sometimes I would even take a look inside. At first my former colleagues thought it was nice. 'Well, hello, old man,' they would laugh, 'can't stay away, can you?' Later, I got the feeling that they were thinking: 'There he is again. What does he want here, anyway?' Now I don't go there anymore. I'm done with it!

"What *is* a human being? What does a human life *mean?* I'm having much difficulty with that. Every day I must pray God to give me strength so I won't become rebellious. Perhaps I'll get used to it. . . ."

"For us women it's a little easier," his wife said. "We aren't suddenly falling from everything into nothing. We may slow down a little when we grow older, but we always keep our occupations."

And again the thought entered my mind: it must be very difficult to be "at rest."

Now I am talking to you. What do *you* think of it? Likely you will agree, more or less, with the remarks of these four talks. Of course, I talked further with all these people. May I summarize my thoughts about these things?

In the first place, I feel that it isn't good to be functioning at peak capacity one day and suddenly to be plunged into a taskless situation the day after the usual farewell party. This abrupt change affects many people so adversely that they do not survive it for any length of time. Others feel that they are without direction and walk "with their souls under their arms."

The housewife, indeed, has it a little easier in these things. As a rule, her task shrinks a little when she grows older and the children leave the house, though she always has enough things to do.

Retirement does not come out of a clear blue sky. You should prepare for it, just as once when you were young you prepared for finding employment.

I always tell older people: work as long as it is day, as long as it is possible. Of course, not as the second person I mentioned above. You are no longer forty or fifty years old. Gradually work should, if at all possible, become a little less. But you ought always to set yourself a task until it is no longer possible. Even then the work of prayer remains as a task. People who always just "sit there doing nothing," as I sometimes observe in some rest homes, are aging rapidly — if not physically, then spiritually. One can always find a task, certainly, if he does not set his goals too high and does not allow money to play too large a role.

Isn't there something to occupy you at home, in the family, in the church, at the neighbor's, among acquaintances who are ill, in the community? Isn't there something for which you can begin to care — even if it may seem insignificant at first?

And then, you should enter your so-called period of retirement as a new *phase of life*, as a new school of learning with new assignments. That period is not just an appendix to your previous life, but the *determining end-phase*. If the Lord grants you the life of a retired person, you must see this as an opportunity, a school of learning.

Look at your retirement and the days of your old age as a school for the aged which prepares you for the eternal life that awaits you. Of course, all of our lives are a preparation for what comes, but you have now come to the *follow-up course*.

Many vocational institutes and technical schools, which prepare their students for a particular task, from time to time recall their graduates who have entered into practice for a refresher course. Experiences are exchanged, errors are discussed and corrected. I believe God intends our old age as such a follow-up course. He takes us apart for a while in a place of restfulness. In that quietness experiences can be exchanged and meditated on, errors and sins can be discovered and confessed and, perhaps, in some cases be set aright.

A South American philosopher has written a book entitled, *Course for Death*. I would like to entitle your old age *Course for Life*.

One who enters the last period of life with this idea will certainly not be bored. On the contrary. He has not entered a dull, monotonous extension, but a new room of life with different furnishings from before. Neither will he (like the second person) remain trotting and toiling as if still forty years old and indispensable. That is an erroneous — and sinful — attitude. Usually, it represents a flight from the end and a failure honestly to

36

admit that we are approaching the moment when we must lay down everything. We should work as though not working. We may not allow our work to bury us. We may not work for the sake of work.

When God calls us to review in the follow-up course, we must come and not pretend that this call is not directed to us. If we reply correctly to his calling voice, we do not complain like the third person mentioned above, and we do not feel as if we are without direction. We overcome our bitter remorse and we prepare for the last round.

And if by and by we cannot "do" a thing anymore — if we should be confined to chair and bed — then there still remains the work of prayer for God's church and for his kingdom and also the work of meditation.

The answer to the question, "How do you like your retirement?" depends in every respect on the answer to the question, "How do you experience this period?"

How do *you* experience it?

7. The Wide-Angle View and the Windshield Wipers

The subject of praying for God's church and his kingdom, which I mentioned toward the end of our previous talk, leads me to something else.

When you have been shunted off the track of labor and production, or when you as a housewife no longer have your family around you, it is understandable that your interests and your field of vision shrink a little. This already begins to happen when the children grow up and leave, no longer storming into your room with their adventures and stories of their experiences. Particularly it affects those who have settled in a home for the aged or a rest home. When you are no longer directly involved with something, your interest wanes visibly. The field of vision becomes smaller.

In some older people I have seen that field of vision become very small indeed. Among them are some who talk about nothing except their ailments — even those which are not too serious.

The other day I visited a lady who had hurt her leg slightly when she had stepped into a car. When I left after forty-five minutes, she had talked only about that little injury. I have also visited older people who talk endlessly about their diet, their insomnia, their appetite or lack of it.

One must watch for the sin of the heart's becoming centered on itself and narrow in its vision. People with a lingering illness are frequently given to such a narrowing of vision. They, too, have been removed from the maelstrom of life and put aside. How tempting it is then to have an eye only for oneself and to pay attention only to one's own difficulties and adversity.

Of course, this variety of egotism simmers in the heart of each of us. But in a Christian this can and must be different. He is able to remain a person with a wide view — even if because of advanced age he no longer gets up out of his chair or bed; even if he is a person who gradually is forgotten by his fellow men.

For instance, when you have not been married and your acquaintances have died, who will come to visit you? I know some of our older fellow-believers who seldom receive visitors in their little rooms.

Yet, even then you don't have to lose the wide angle view, not even when your daily view is nothing more than four walls in a small room and one tree in front of a window: *if you only pray* — and pray profitably.

This means — as we said in the last talk — that you pray for the coming of God's kingdom, for the welfare of his church and similar matters of concern. By praying you travel the world. You visit the mission fields and the evangelism stations. You bring everything you come across to the Lord in prayer. This way it is impossible for your vision to become narrow or a feeling of purposelessness to overwhelm you. Isn't the praying home front of the greatest importance? When Moses' hands pointed prayerfully to heaven, Amalek lost and Israel won the battle (Exodus 17). Someone put it this way: God rules the world not from the conference centers of world powers, but from attic rooms and sickbeds in which prayers are offered.

Your angle of vision remains wide, too, *when you have faith*. Through faith, in fact, your angle becomes wider than the world. You not only have a worldwide view — which is quite large already — but you also have a "heavenly view." Was it not in faith that Abraham saw from afar the city which has foundations, whose builder and maker is God (Hebrews 11:10) — the new Jerusalem? And Paul the Apostle in prison, suffering and growing older, did not only look to the things that are visible, but also to the unseen (2 Corinthians 4). By faith, God's children retain a wide-angle view when they grow old. They do not stare at a black wall or into a dark pit: they keep the everlasting heavens in sight. In the words of Isaac Watts:

> We see the Canaan that we love,
>> With faith's illumined eyes:
> By faith we climb where Moses stood,
>> And view the landscape o'er,
> Not Jordan's stream, nor death's cold flood,
>> Should fright us from the shore!

My thoughts go for a moment to the dedication service for a new Christian school in a little Dutch village. Through the large windows of the new building one had a wide-angle view of tracts of rich land reclaimed from water and of blue lakes.

A government inspector, obviously someone who thought Christianity to be too narrow and choking, made a congratulatory speech in which he urged the teaching staff to mold the minds of their pupils by giving them a wide-angle view such as these windows inspired.

In my reply I assured the inspector that this school certainly would train people to have a wide-angle view. Not because of all those windows, but because it was a Bible-centered Christian school. If the Bible governs our education, our eyes will be opened to things others barely see and scarcely suspect to exist.

But I must return to those windows for a moment. Windows can steam up from the inside and be blurred by rain on the outside. Under such conditions one hardly has any view at all. Windows become almost like frosted glass. So, too, the windows to our souls can easily become steamed up or blurred by rain.

Before we realize what is happening, discouragement, sorrow and sin steam up our souls' windows. Like a driving rain, adversity and life's problems beat against them.

Whenever one's view is obstructed while driving a car, he turns on the windshield wiper. Something like this is necessary in spiritual traffic too. Our life speeds toward the end. "We fly away."

Keep the windows of your soul clean.

Keep your view unobstructed.

Keep your wide-angle view, lest accidents — spiritual collisions and injuries — occur.

Then turn on the windshield wipers. That is, take care of your spiritual life thoughtfully and carefully. Maintain your reading habit. Pray without ceasing.

"Let us be *always* hopeful, prayerful, watchful, strengthen each other in the faith."

8. The Gift of Silence

Silence please; on crystal feet
silence strides into our night
like a snowflake sending greetings
from above to our lone watch.

The poem sings the praise of silence; maybe not the way you would say it, but there is much truth in these lines. Silence brings to our ear sounds and voices we may not hear at other times.

In the silence we begin to understand the whisperings of the soul. God's speaking in his Word gets really through to us only in a milieu of silence. A buzzing, bustling church service, for instance, does not do as much justice to the Word of God as a silent, reverent hour of worship. Silence is a gift.

Often I am reminded of that when I come to visit older persons. How quiet the room frequently is! Even the halls in many rest homes breathe this atmosphere.

This silence is all the more noticeable now that

everything outside has become so busy and helter-skelter. Traffic roars by. At the office typewriters and calculators rattle. In factories turbines drone. In living rooms radios and television sets scream, accompanied by the whine of the vacuum cleaner. Amid all these noises I sometimes retreat into the church building to be surrounded by silence and to think for a moment.

I also find that silence and serenity surrounding many of you. Often I find you in your room sitting in front of the window with a book, a magazine, or something to knit or embroider — in silence.

Is silence a gift for you?

Silence can become an obsession. When that happens, we want to see *people*. We want to have noise around us. But here again, it depends on how we accept and experience silence. Isn't it wonderful to let all the busyness of life pass you by and enjoy peace and silence? Superficial, empty people do not know the silence. It is no compliment to our times if peace and quiet disappear altogether, evaporating into uproariousness. A poem by Scheltema is to the point:

> people who fear every silence
> never must have read their hearts
> never must have bent their knees.

In the biography of a Dutch educator who retired at the early age of 58 to find silence in a peaceful hamlet, the author says:

> It was not surprising to him that sometimes strong people could not be found, because silent people are strong people and they are trained to be strong only in hours of silence — but today people no longer have silent moments.

43

Indeed, the truly great have known and loved the silence. Moses spent forty years in the silence of the deserts. He was equipped for his enormous task of leading Israel out of Egypt even more in the desert than he would have been in the busy activity of Pharaoh's court, where he grew up.

Was it the worst time of David's life when he was a shepherd boy in the silence of the fields? How many psalms didn't he compose there!

Elijah, rebellious and discouraged, finds his peace with God in the desert near Mount Horeb — in the soft, singing silence and the still, small voice.

Until the day of his public appearance in Israel, John the Baptist spent his days in silence in the desert.

Between the time of his conversion and his public appearance, Paul spent three years in the desert of Arabia.

On the quiet island of Patmos, John had his visions.

Jesus himself repeatedly sought the mountaintops for prayer and meditation.

The active Luther once said to his fellow Reformer, the even more active Melanchthon, "One must sometimes be able to be lazy for the glory of God."

And so it is. Silence is a gift. From time to time all of us must be surrounded by it, or our life will become hollow.

The closer we draw to the gate that leads to eternity, the more necessary it is for us to spend time in silence!

Of course this does not mean that you should completely dissociate yourself from life because it's too busy. Certainly not. No matter how old you get, you must maintain an interest in life.

In the Middle Ages, Sister Bertke had masons enclose her within the walls of a church in Utrecht so that she could be secluded from the world. I believe this was a mistake. It would be an equally serious mistake for you to turn your room into such a retreat. The windows to everyday life must remain open as long as possible. But this does not take away the fact that silence may and should have a place in your life.

Some years ago a book was published in Holland with the title *Talks with Yourself*. I wonder how many people who have come to an advanced age have ever really had a good talk with themselves.

Have you ever listened attentively to the voices of your own heart? Do you really know what has always motivated you? What drove you onward?

As I am writing this, a daily newspaper has begun to ask prominent personalities: what was the most beautiful day in your life? Several of the celebrities really have no idea how to answer that question. Do you? Or is the most beautiful day still forthcoming?

In this way you may be busy with yourself in silence. Your thoughts may go out to your husband, your wife, your children, your friends, your work, your church and its relationship to you.

Above all, in that silence one can listen particularly well to God's Word.

I often meet elderly people who keep a Bible very close to themselves. To them the words appear new time and again. Special texts, familiar to the reader at this age, may in the silence of the day sometimes speak differently and more urgently than before. The Bible repeatedly speaks in a peculiar way to appropriate points of time in our lives, and also in the several phases of our lives.

The Lord places quiet times on your agenda. Use silence well. For in silence the song of praise is born.

9. Night Terrors

While I was talking about silence, I recalled visits at which I was greeted with a sigh, "I didn't sleep very well again last night. Never shut an eye, Pastor."

According to a survey two of five women and one of five men don't sleep very well.

I have on occasion casually noted that even the Bible talks about old people who "rise up at the voice of a bird" (Ecclesiastes 12:4).

Young people can usually sleep through everything; indeed, their parents sometimes have great difficulty getting them out of bed in the morning. Older people, on the other hand, are often already awake when a bird whistles in the attic window. At the same time they may be suffering from insomnia. How troublesome those nights can be! You turn and turn and nothing helps. You just stay awake. You've counted all the chimes, every dragging hour, and time does not seem to move. Darkness keeps surrounding you. Finally, you get weary of twisting and turning.

But not only that. In those wakeful nights many

thoughts haunt your mind. Everything appears gloomy, frightful, and dark. The future, or your own condition — anything about which you could think rationally and quietly during the day — now agonizes you. These things now occur to you as what psychologists might refer to as *night terrors*. "The terror of the night," the Bible calls it (Psalm 91:5).

Night terrors make everything we perceive more frightening. I remember well how afraid I would be as a boy when heavy thunderstorms would strike during the night. The same claps of thunder during the daytime would find me sitting quietly in front of a window, looking at the lightning. How many times have you lain in bed worrying in your sleeplessness and have anxiously wondered about all kinds of things?

One shouldn't lightly pass over such anxieties. "And then I take another sleeping pill," the insomniac may say. Of course, you can resort to such means for relief. But don't let it be your only refuge. You must also ask yourself if your sleeplessness may have a cause. Taking sleeping pills without trying to find the cause of your insomnia is like mopping up a floor while running water onto it. It doesn't help at all!

Maybe the Bible can help us find possible causes. The text we quoted above presents your insomnia as a natural event that accompanies old age.

You are working less, move around less. For you the contrast between day and night is not so much in terms of work and rest as in terms of light and darkness.

Sometimes people are startled by my visiting their rooms when they are dozing off — during the daytime. The division between being awake and being asleep is less distinguishable than before. It goes without saying, then, that one may sleep more lightly and fewer hours during the night.

I am thinking of another text too. This one goes: "In the night also my heart instructs me" (Psalm 16:7).

Today we might say: the subconscious surfaced. In the Bible the heart was the seat of the deepest feelings and the most hidden motives. When the Bible says that God knows the hearts of all men, it means that God knows us through and through, better than we know ourselves.

It is very possible that you or I, in our conscious living and thinking, have not set aside a place for various things. We may have pushed these out of our thoughts. Such things go down into our subconscious. But when we sleep, things that have been pushed aside surface again. Then, "in the night my heart instructs me." We wake up and do not easily fall asleep again. And often we are unaware of what is happening — we may stay awake out of a subconscious fear that these cellar-like thoughts will resurface. Disturbances of sleep can be (though they are not always) an alarm signaling that something is not in order in our spiritual lives. For example, when I have been severely irritated about something during the daytime, chances are that these repressed irritations will awaken me at night, because at night my heart begins to speak.

I mentioned repressed irritations. Concealed guilt feelings can be the reason for these, as can repressed fear of death.

I believe that fear of death plays a larger role in an elderly person than you may suspect. One who approaches the door to eternity thinks more about death. Yet I must say that I don't hear aged people speak quite as often about death as younger people do. Death is being suppressed. But during the night this makes itself felt. Unsolved problems and unresolved questions of life and death assert themselves during the night. Marie

Post has caught the essence of these experiences in her poem, "Awake at Night":

> Restlessly the wind turns
> On the vast, uneasy bed of night
> (As I turn on my hard-pillowed bed
> In this dark and shadowed room)
> Moaning the same questions
> Over and over and finding (as I do)
> The same unacceptable answers.

Repressed questions appear as night terrors, more frightful and harrowing. Many a night terror can be traced to a fear of death.

The noted Swiss psychiatrist Carl G. Jung said that he found fear of death at the bottom of every soul — even in people who speak indifferently about dying. Hebrews 2:14 speaks of those "who through fear of death were subject to lifelong bondage." Could this, along with other matters, be the cause of your sleeplessness?

Many psychiatrists assume that such an ailment will be removed if one just knows its cause. If you discover what accounts for your sleeplessness, restful sleep will return to you. I disagree in this case. I do not believe that knowing the cause is also the cure. Knowledge does not always mean power. You must also resolve the cause.

How rich the Christian faith then makes you! You must be active with that faith. Live in that faith. Sleep in that faith, as the prophet once did: "My soul yearns for thee in the night, my spirit within me earnestly seeks thee" (Isaiah 26:9).

Keep the Lord always in your vision, during sleepless nights too. He is near you as the Resurrected One! In his presence the deepest threat of the fear of death falls away. At best only something of a biological fear, a natural shiver over something unusual, remains.

Do not just think "beautiful thoughts." Envision Jesus himself as the conqueror standing before you. His perfect love shuts out fear.

A certain order of nuns, before retiring to bed in their dark rooms, must make a cross over the bed. Then they lay down with the prayer: "Into your hands I commend my spirit."

Falling asleep indeed has something of the falling asleep as in death. Falling asleep is an undoing of the affairs and cares of the life lived in wakefulness. Often, one who cannot and does not want to die, even though he stands near the door of eternity, will have difficulty falling asleep at night. He cannot undo the cares of the day.

Why not then commend your spirit to him who lives in all eternity, and who gives life to his own.

Then you can sing:

> Peacefully I fell asleep,
> aware of God's faithfulness,
> till, refreshed, I awakened,
> *For God was at my side.*

Are night terrors frightening you?

Why not read Psalm 92:1-2, "It is good . . . to declare . . . thy faithfulness by night," and Psalm 91:1, "He who dwells in the shelter of the Most High, *abides* in the shadow of the Almighty." And then find sleep, in complete surrender of your whole being in him: "Into your hands I commend my spirit."

We close with a poem by R. Houwink called "Before Falling Asleep":

I must close my eyes
and entrust myself.
I cannot do otherwise
than fold my hands
and board ship,
bravely board ship
on the ocean
of your mercy,
and say this:
No, Lord, you cannot mean
that this night
is the eternal end
and your sun
shall rise
nevermore
before my eyes
not yet satisfied;
and
nevermore your word
may feed
indestructible homesickness
of this heart
for you.

10. "Absalom, My Son, Absalom..."

I always find the biblical story of Absalom's death (2 Samuel 18-19) a very moving one. Its climax is the old father David's bewilderment. His cry of distress so deeply affects even the calloused soldiers that they slip stealthily through the city gates under the cries of the king who moans in the tower room, "Absalom, my son! My son Absalom! Would I had died instead of you...."

In that moan I always hear reproach. A son has died in his sins. The father knows that he shares the guilt of this horrible end: would I had died instead of you.... As is well known, David suffers in Absalom's death the consequences of his own sins of years before.

I mention this story because so many people growing and grown old are weighed down by past sins and their consequences. I am not asserting that you do not have your present sins. Alas! we remain sinners-in-action till the last breath. Old age even has its own peculiar sins. But it seems as though the devil takes special pleasure in rubbing these sins of the past into our consciousness. And the consequences of these sins may remind us of other, earlier transgressions.

But we cannot simply wash our hands in innocence, and the longer our lives the longer the list of our sins grows.

When Jesus said, after the adulteress had been dragged before him, "Whosoever is without sin, let him cast the first stone" (John 8:7), the Pharisees left, one by one. But have you ever noticed the rest of the sentence, "... beginning with the *oldest?*" Did they have the most wrongdoings on their conscience?

Several visits and conversations now come to my mind. I think of an aged couple, whose evening of life was darkened by the thought of a prodigal son. "He doesn't participate in anything, Pastor. He doesn't even pray anymore. He lives like a pagan. But we ... we spoiled him. He was our only son. We had made an idol of him. And now God has pushed our idol off its pedestal. ... We would rather have lost our son to death than to lose him this way!"

I also think of that old brother, a faithful church-goer, who never participated in holy communion. When he was asked why he did not take communion, his answer always boiled down to, "I didn't feel free to do so."

When we had become more friendly and better acquainted, he suddenly burst out one day, "I'll tell you honestly what keeps me from taking communion. When I was young I betrayed the love of a girl. And then she committed suicide. She ran out of the house and drowned herself. I've decided, then, not to let it bother me. I've even been fairly happily married. But now that I am old and left behind, this haunts me every day. And at night I lay awake because of that. ..."

I also think of the grey-haired man who had deserted

wife and children many years ago. And after that, for a time, he had given his love to someone else, without being married to her. He did not admit that this was wrong, this old, faithful churchgoer. His first wife was at fault, he thought. With a gentle persuasion I pushed him, each time, into the direction of "the way back." It didn't work. Admission of guilt becomes more and more difficult as one grows older.

Old, hardened trees bend only with great difficulty. One loses so much prestige on the outside; must it also be given up on the inside, spiritually? Should younger people, whom you've had on your knees when they were children, hear you tell them that you've been mistaken and have sinned in many respects?

But behind all his rationalizations this man hid a consciousness of guilt. From his deathbed he wrote a note to his wife and children asking if they would come. After twenty years they saw each other again. I will never forget this togetherness. Late, but not too late, they confessed their guilt to each other and were reconciled. . . .

I think, too, of a man whose doctor had given him no hope for recovery. Already he had been set aside in a small room in the hospital. It was late in the evening when I was called to his bedside. When I saw him, I knew he would not make it through the night. I had never before been mistaken when I had made that judgment about a seriously ill person, but this time I was wrong. The man perked up and lived through the crisis. Later I told him how I had misjudged his end. "I understand," he said, "I would have died. But I could not die. I never had talked. . . ." I looked at him puzzled. "Yes — you see, I mean I have never spoken of *him!* Not even to my own children. I've talked about everything, but never about *him.* That thought startled me. And I felt my guilt so acutely, that I pleaded: let me still live, Lord. I cannot die. . . ." The man lived another short year and turned his bed into a pulpit.

I think of the woman who fell crying on her knees when her husband breathed his last breath: "O God, God, I'm such a miserable person. . . ." She literally screamed. During the first moments that followed, she could not be calmed down. All her regrets about the shortcomings in her life towards this man (though it had been a "respectable" marriage) burst out in these wails.

How many widowers and widows do not walk around with a continuous, "If I had only. . . ."

I think of St. Augustine, who had the walls of the room in which he was dying pasted full with psalms of penitence. Then he wished to be left alone, amidst these psalms.

I think of John Calvin, who called the city fathers of Geneva to his deathbed and asked them to forgive his sharp outbursts.

I think — but I shall not mention more. But how are these things with you?

Our sins may, just before the door to eternity, give us a difficult time. Satan often stacks them up before us into quite a mountain, a mountain we can no longer look over.

Will there yet be grace for me?

Will I be allowed to enter?

These questions arise in our anxiety. The devil tries his best as he makes his last attempts to pull us away from that door.

One solution presents itself, the solution that the hymn suggests:

> May then your blood kindle my hope
> And cover my guilt before God.

Once I read this story about a dream Martin Luther had. The end was near. Satan pushed a large sheet of paper in front of Luther. On the paper some of Luther's misdeeds were written.

"Do you know any more?" Luther asked.

"Yes," Satan said.

"Then add these." The misdeeds were added.

"Don't you know any more sins?"

"Yes, there are still some things."

"Then write everything down." It was done.

By now the sheet had been completely filled.

"All right," Luther said. He added more to his list of sins. Then he took a pen dipped in red ink and wrote across the page: "His blood cleanses from all sins."

When he looked up, Satan had disappeared.

He took the paper, tore it up, and awoke rejoicing.

To our complaint, "Do not remember the sins of my youth . . . do not remember the evil we committed," the answer sounds forth: "I am a complete remission for all your sins. Only believe."

> Here, O my Lord, I see thee face to face;
> Here would I touch and handle things unseen;
> Here grasp with firmer hand eternal grace,
> And all my weariness upon thee lean.
>
> I have no help but thine; nor do I need
> Another arm save thine to lean upon;
> It is enough, my Lord, enough indeed;
> My strength is in thy might, thy might alone.
> — *Horatius Bonar, 1855*

11. I Dreamed

Old age certainly is not the time of the fewest dreams. For good reason the Bible talks about old people dreaming dreams (Joel 2:28). Though specific dreams are meant here, preoccupation with dreams is admittedly one of older people in particular.

A friendly, good-natured woman often tells me, "Pastor, I have such beautiful dreams. In my dreams I'm home again with my mother. I play behind the old house. And again I find myself in the classroom as a pupil of my teacher." She is not the only one who has told me of having such dreams.

Why don't we accept these dreams as a friendly gift from God? Much of what has fallen away during the years, many loved ones and dear ones, return to you in this way for a short while. You may look upon these dreams as flowers blooming from the wilting branches of the trees of your life. There is a beautiful poem by Hélène Swarth:

The pale morning slipped away with the dew,

> The grey afternoon stretches its slow, weary limbs.
> I stretch out longing arms toward the night.
> So calmly, happily, I lay my hands into your hands,
> O night! Lead me to distant lands of dreams.

Yet, upon your awakening, something painful emerges from such dreams. The dear ones with whom you have visited for a moment, as though they still were alive, have vanished, and you sit there alone amidst the hard life of your old age, with its worries and sorrow. Involuntarily you may sigh: how many loved ones have fallen away; how small the circle of relatives and friends has grown. They are like leaves falling off the trees in autumn: fewer and fewer remain on the branches, until finally one sees only a single, lonesome leaf on some of the twigs. Isaiah says it so strikingly: "We all fade like a leaf" (64:6). But when you awaken, think rather of this beautiful verse:

> Sometimes on life's pathway
> God's fatherly hand
> ties a heart to our heart,
> lends a hand to our hands.
>
> One here and one yonder,
> and many a time
> we don't meet each other
> on the earth again.
>
> But again we meet dear ones
> who found the great Friend,
> the oldest and dearest,
> the strongest, most faithful
> redeemer of men.

An old lady once said to me, "You should hear this. I've had such a peculiar dream. I saw a narrow door. I couldn't get through the opening. But suddenly I felt myself growing light and slender. At that moment I was on the other side. My feet were trembling. I covered my eyes with my hands. It was as if I stood in a radiant snowscape in which diamonds sparkled at my feet. I glanced at my clothes. They had become grey and dirty. Suddenly I felt myself being lifted up. I was gliding along white walls and over green palm trees. An angel carried me. 'Let go of me!' I cried. 'No, I can't,' he said, 'we're going to the white throne. Do you see those beaming rays up yonder?' Startled, I lost consciousness. When I came to, I stood among a great multitude dressed in white robes. As I opened my eyes I saw the Lord Jesus standing before me. Pastor, it really was as if he was there. Yes, it *was* he. He handed me a palm branch and said, 'Enter, you blessed of the father. . . .'

"I could hear that voice so clearly in my ears that it woke me up. I'd say he stood by my bed. What do you think of this, Pastor? May I believe that one day I shall be admitted into heaven?"

Perhaps you too have had a dream similar to this one. Are you wondering what I have to say about that? Of course, I am not going to say that one can *only* be assured of salvation when he has experienced such voices and such dreams. I do not find that as a condition for salvation in the Bible. The Scriptures *do* say that one cannot see God without faith and sanctification. And I am committed to the service of the Word of God, which binds men to its conditions and promises.

On the other hand, I cannot throw such a dream out of the window as useless or deceptive. I believe the Lord is able to use such dreams to strengthen our faith, even if I cannot accept the lady's idea that Jesus himself stood by her bed and spoke to her.

All kinds of thoughts that occupy a person's soul are

revealed symbolically in dreams. Doubt, certainty, and a degree of resistance appear to occupy the soul of this lady dreamer, but certainty appears to be dominant.

This is a dream that relates to the future. Whenever you dream like this you are, more than you realize, struggling with the last things and with what is yet to come. A dream such as this may be accepted as a comfort from God's hand. By visions of the night God may also speak his word to us or confirm his word.

Aged persons may also dream of their funerals. They may experience in these dreams everything that they expect will happen at that time until, wet with perspiration, they awake. Usually these people think that after such a dream death is impending at any moment. But this somber expectation is not in fact often followed by death itself. These dreams betray fear of death and they relate to unsolved problems that occupy a person's spirit.

These dreams call you to make a clean slate with these questions. They invite you not to leave them wandering in your mind as unsolved mysteries.

Here the word Isaiah brought to King Hezekiah applies: "Set your house in order, for you shall die" (2 Kings 20:1). The more peaceful the state of the soul is, so are the dreams also calm. To a soul in that condition dreams turn into an enjoyment and a comfort.

The past and the future present themselves to our vision. Yesterday, today, and tomorrow blend into one view.

12. Light Spots

When Naomi returned from the land of Moab, she brought back a life of grief and sadness. She had left filled, she came back empty.

A blossoming, happy woman emigrated; an emaciated, gloomy, dejected woman returned. "Is this really *Naomi?*" the women wondered, staring at her from behind the drapes at their windows. "Do not call me *Naomi,* call me *Mara,*" she said. Mara — bitterness. . . .

Persons who have not seen you for many years may be startled when they come to visit you: grey, thinner, obviously grown old. But don't let them hear you say, as I have heard from old mouths more than once, "Call me Mara, because my life turned out to be a chunk of bitterness. There's nothing left of me!"

Who would deny that old age brings with it infirmities? Who would deny that to many it means loneliness, desertion, and grief? "Laughter belongs to the young, complaint to the old."

And yet. . . .

Old age is like a dark forest. The sun creates count-less light spots through the branches and leaves. In the lives of older people, too, such light spots shine through. Let's talk about some of these.

First, you enjoy the privilege that *you have come to stand behind things*. You will have a better vision of many matters from this vantage point than when you were in the middle of things. Now you see your life in perspective, with dimension, as in a painting you look at from a distance.

The book *The Great Hall* (we mentioned it earlier in our third talk) describes how an old woman ends up in a rest home. Consequently, her furniture has to be sold. When she is told as gently and carefully as possible that she must sell her furniture, she sees her possessions before her mind's eye. Among them is a dresser with a spot burned in it. She recalls how angry she had been with her husband that day when he had let his cigar fall out of the ashtray onto the dresser. She had nagged him about it all day. How small-minded this seems to her in retrospect. If she only still had her Bill, she wouldn't mind if he burned the whole dresser!

After our sixties we begin to see things more and more in their true proportions. Things that seemed so large become small and the things that seemed so small become large! We find ourselves behind the events. . . .

Next, we may appreciate as a bright side of old age that *our memory revives our youth*. We've already talked about the sins of that period in our lives; the sins that we often see more clearly now than we did then. But there is also a beautiful side to reliving one's youth. Someone has written that it is the memory of youth which can give old age such a lovely cast. "That memory enlightens the somewhat somber seriousness of youth with the love of our parents, the intimacy of the home we grew up in, the familiar give-and-take with brothers, sisters, and other relatives, with child's play, and the light cast on our lives from the first tugs we felt of the love of our God and from the answer to that love in our child-like prayers. O youth! . . . All of its experiences return to us when we grow old."

If we avoid idealizing the past, the memory of youth certainly can shed a beam of light over our old age.

A third light spot is that *you do not have to participate in the speed and the noise of everyday life.* In the morning, when everyone rushes to work, no matter the weather, you may begin your day at a quiet pace. You have a little more chance to be yourself. You may develop talents that remained dormant during the years in which your daily work required all of your energies. How many women of sixty years and older — and this was already the case in the days of St. Paul — devote themselves to all sorts of work in church and society when the children are grown up and have left the home. And I have found that retired schoolteachers are among the best gardeners in backyards they formerly neglected.

In this period of rest you may also meditate, read, walk, or do many other things.

Freedom from many kinds of worry and concerns is certainly a bright spot in the dark forest of old age. What a peaceful thought to know that the children have arrived at their destination. What a blessing for Christian parents to see as their children mature that they join heartily in the activities of God's kingdom. My father wrote these words from John's letters in the Bible my parents gave me years ago: "I know no greater joy than this, that my children walk in the truth." The deepest joy beams over our life when we see that the Lord goes from generation to generation. In the Bible this is presented as a shout of joy: *he saw his children's children!*

One who grows old is able to see that God's work in church, life, and world does not stand or fall depending on a certain person, but that he continues his work, even when you fall away. One who has not sought his own selfish pursuits can rejoice about that.

May I mention just one more bright spot — one of the most beautiful? When my aged father died, a colleague wrote to me: the old generation has now fallen away. Now you are joining that generation. Now you are moving up to the front line. But *from that vantage point you can see better*. In old age we stand closer to the route along which the King comes. The older one gets, the nearer to Jesus.

Every day brings us nearer to him. We yearn more and more for the heavenly mansion, as the song says. When we find that yearning in ourselves, the evening of our life may, if only for that reason, be bright.

13. Danger Ahead

Does old age not know danger and worry? It certainly does. It would be too idealistic of us only to blow the trumpet of praise for old age. Any period in one's lifetime brings its own particular exposure to certain dangers.

Let me mention some of them briefly in this conversation. A number of the following points are discussed in more detail in other conversations in this book, but perhaps it will be useful to summarize them here.

• Do not pride yourself on what you consider to be some beautiful role you have played in the past. You would not do such a thing out of wisdom, the writer of Ecclesiastes says.

• Do not reject out of hand everything or much that belongs to this present time.

• Do not become egoistic and self-centered.

• Do not allow yourself to be buried in grief about lost dear ones. Do not talk about your losses in every conversation and with everyone you meet.

• Do not become stifled by your loneliness.

• Do not become too relativistic in your outlook. This

may give rise to a negative attitude that doesn't want to get involved in anything, but that dismisses ideas cynically with a remark like "Don't get so excited; I've learned that it doesn't help at all."

• Do not become greedy.
• Do not grow bitter.
• Do not lose sight of your surroundings; remain involved.
• Do not become a compulsive talker.
• Do not push away all thoughts of death and dying.
• Persevere till the end.

Paul's suggestions were to the point: "Bid the older men be temperate, serious, sensible, sound in faith, in love, and in steadfastness.

"Bid the older women, likewise, to be reverent in behavior, not to be slanderers or slaves to drink; they are to teach what is good" (Titus 2:2-3).

The Bible has many examples of people who in their old age fell into sin. But on the other hand the promise is clear: "Be faithful unto death, and I will give you the crown of life" (Revelation 2:10).

14. Wrinkles

I know someone who, as he grew older, experienced much difficulty and grief. He missed love and an environment of acceptance. On his desk he put a photograph of a very old woman. Her face seemed one big wrinkle. But from each wrinkle in her face a little wave of friendliness rippled. And the crows' feet around the eyes gave an almost roguish impression. Many cares had moved across that face, but she had kept her courage. Her friendliness had gained in depth. How open and warm and wise was this face. The man who put this portrait on his desk felt encouraged and strengthened each time he looked at the old woman.

I think, too, of the portrait Rembrandt painted of his mother. How strikingly he shows the detail of veins and wrinkles in her hands. They concentrate on an open Bible. She had to let go of much, but not of this. These hands had never seen a manicurist, yet how beautiful they are.

After seeing this painting, you may find ironic much of today's advertising for cosmetics, with its suggestion that beauty is only found in the smooth and clear skin of the fashion model, carefully ministered to with various creams, lotions, and exotic preparations.

Of course I do not mean to suggest that you should no longer take care of yourself and how you look. On the contrary, I believe that in growing older you must pay even more attention to grooming and appearance. Thus renewed attention is necessary because it is so easy for an older person to neglect himself. "They don't look at you anymore." "You don't rate anymore." "I'm not going out of the house today, anyway."

When one has reached an even more advanced age, this excuse is added: "Why should I still buy something new? I don't wear out any clothes; the old ones are still good enough." Not everyone has the vitality of an old grandfather I knew who wanted to be fitted for a new winter coat in his ninetieth year.

"Should you really do that?" one of his daughters offered carefully. "You may be wearing it for such a short time. . . ."

"You said the same thing ten years ago when I wanted to buy a bicycle," he retorted. And the new winter coat has already served him for eight years.

There can be a practical reason, too. At an advanced age, one is more likely to spill food and drink on his clothes. His hands become unsteady, sometimes slightly jittery. He does not see so well anymore. This, too, is among the reasons you should be doubly attentive to your appearance.

In my pastoral rounds I visit with two women who live in adjoining rooms. The one is nearly blind, yet she is always walking into her neighbor's room to ask: "Say, would you look to see if there are any stains on my clothes?" That is the way it should be. A Christian, who knows himself or herself to be an image-bearer of God, must take care of his or her appearance. One who prays for a clean heart should not walk around unclean and clothes dappled with stains.

But that does not mean that we go to extremes to remove every little wrinkle from our faces. It does not mean that we do all we can to look as young as possible.

That appears to be the trend of our time. It almost seems as if people consider it a *duty* for everyone to look young. Not too many years ago, the exact opposite was the case: young people dressed like older people in order to be accepted among the grownups and to be counted.

I read recently of a sixty-year-old European woman who emigrated to the U.S.A. Though she spared no effort, she had a great deal of difficulty finding work. A theater owner gave her a temporary job as a cashier. When she had worked there for a week, her boss said, "I'd like to take you on permanently, but only after you pay a visit to a beauty parlor!"

"In the beauty parlor they dyed and curled my hair," she writes, "and the beautician put a golden hairband on my head. They worked and worked on my face and then painted my fingernails fire-engine red. I feel like a baboon, or rather, like a woman of seventy years old who wants to look like forty. But my boss is very satisfied.

"This need to appear young is no longer a pleasure; it is a solemn duty. If you don't participate in the latest fashionable look, you're a wet blanket and are ostracized."

I am inclined to say: better a wet blanket than a stuffed bird in a cage! One cannot help asking, how does this need come about? Why do people, no matter what the cost, want to look young and without wrinkles?

Many factors could be mentioned. But the most important factor is this one, that people no longer appear to be living by the message of that verse we have quoted several times: "As I draw nearer to the house of my Father...." People no longer appear to know to whom and to what they draw nearer: whether darkness, doom, going-down, nothingness, light, or God.

Samuel Beckett's play *Waiting for Godot* summarizes starkly the plight of many people today. The drama consists entirely of a dialogue between two wanderers who are waiting for a certain person who has promised to come, but of whom they know nothing except that his name is Godot. As they wait, the two men talk and talk some more, and each time the message comes: Godot has again been prevented from coming!

In these idle wanderers — of which Paris and many other large cities know hundreds — wanderers who dwell and sleep under the bridges, doing nothing and waiting for someone who does not come and who perhaps actually does not really exist, the playwright wanted to portray modern man.

In such uncertainty it is difficult, if not impossible, to advance courageously. When someone finds himself in a mountain range amidst canyons and ravines, snow and ice, and he does not know where he is about to step, involuntarily that person stands still. When in life with its questions and darkness, its mountains and canyons, I do not know what point I will come to, I am also standing still.

And so it is that people today hang on for dear life to their youth, to the blossom of life. One wants to cling to the temporal life, because he does not know the permanence of life anymore, and is afraid to face anything definite. The *now,* the moment, is elevated at the expense of the *then,* the eternal, the future.

You ought not to participate in this youth culture! If you are a believer, the word once spoken by Daniel in the evening of his life applies to you: "But go your way till the end; and you shall rest, and shall stand in your allotted place at the end of the days" (Daniel 12:13). Daniel isn't threatened with some dark abyss, or with nothingness, or with something like that. No, he is told that he will arrive at his destination at the end of the days. In the New Testament, of course, this promise is depicted in even greater clarity. John in Revelation sees visions of a new Jerusalem. Whoever believes is on his way to glory. And so, for you, this life is but a preparation.

You may write above your life, as Erasmus of Rotterdam did, *nondum*, "not yet." "Truly life and love and blessing is seen there where Jesus is."

I should, therefore, not hold tightly to anything in this life. On the contrary, I am to possess all as if not possessing. For that reason do not take an active part in today's youth culture. Actually that culture is a little laughable anyway. When people take a close look, they will certainly notice that you're no longer in your thirties or forties. If you pretend you are, you really only succeed in making yourself a little ridiculous.

Think once of how you react to precocious children and young people who speak as though they have the wisdom of age. Isn't it boring, dissonant, unreal to listen to them? Don't present a reverse picture, one which is even more ridiculous and boring.

Dress well and neatly, but don't be afraid to admit in your choice of clothing that you are no longer sweet sixteen. You need not accentuate in your dress that you aren't as young as you used to be, yet when people praise or flatter you that you are still looking *so* young, remember that this is the best evidence that you *are not* so young anymore. They didn't say that when you really were seventeen!

Accept your age, along with its bright and shadowy sides. When you do that, these years will not fail to enrich your life uncommonly. In faith, go your way till the end. Do not make hopeless, spasmodic attempts to stand still and remain young.

You are not as old as you feel. Nor are you "as old as your arteries." You are as old as your number of years, and these years are counted and known by God and by yourself.

Mature, calm people *are* "beautiful" people, even with their wrinkles.

positive? You ask yourself, how do they behave in my presence? But you should also ask yourself, how do I behave in their presence? Believe me, they are watching you. And you may count on it that young people also feel they find fault and sin among older people. I often hear young people say, "Those old people really take things easy; they are willing to leave injustices the way they are. If something is unjust, you should speak up and act against it, but they are afraid of a little uneasiness messing up their quiet life. They're much too fond of their conveniences, and of their comforts."

And young people even charge older ones with superficiality and frivolousness. There's a German folk ditty that goes something like this:

> As a boy defiant, tried everything,
> As a young man pretentious and taken aback,
> As a man ready for action,
> As an old man frivolous and capricious.
> On his tombstone one will be reading:
> He truly was a human being.

Usually such old folk rhymes contain an element of truth. In any event, you should first take a good look at yourself and ask, what good am I to younger persons? Do I mean anything positive to them?

Concerning money, Paul has said that "children ought not to lay up for their parents, but parents for their children" (2 Corinthians 12:14). This certainly applies also to spiritual things. What have you gathered in the way of spiritual capital in the course of the years? What do you offer young people of that capital?

In this connection, take a close look at that little letter of St. Paul to Philemon. Paul was old when he wrote that letter. Notice how he speaks about the young

Onesimus. "My child," "my very heart," he calls this young man. Consider that Onesimus was really a runaway slave — in the eyes of that time not a very good child. Also notice in how friendly and appreciative a manner Paul addresses Philemon. As an older person he could perhaps have commanded Philemon to do what was required, but instead Paul makes a friendly request. Look, this is a positive, uplifting attitude. One who approaches youth in this manner becomes the friend and the source of information for youth.

I know that in the industrialized world of today the aged person is no longer a reference book for the young. Young people no longer learn their trades from their fathers, but at vocational schools and colleges.

Fine. But this is not yet true with respect to spiritual matters. A single conversation with an older, wiser brother or sister can mean far more than studying thick books full of knowledge.

Ask for God's grace and assistance to be such a guide. Do not look on critically, bitter and irritated. Be so involved with life that younger people like to sit down with you to have a good talk. Grandparents can be a great blessing for their grandchildren especially if the fathers and mothers, because of the busyness of their own lives, do not get to talk to their children as much as they should.

I know some older persons at whose homes I frequently find young people visiting. And these young people always take something with them; they come out wiser than they came in. You can mean much to the young soul which often goes through crises, with your wider, milder view and your wealth of experience. I think back with gratitude to an afternoon I spent as a young student in the study of an old emeritus minister.

Such people I would like to call *pilgrim attractions for youth*. Gladly I send young people to their homes.

More and more older people are retaining their physical fitness and lively disposition for a longer time. They participate in all kinds of activities. And they are by no means out of it. But where are the pilgrim attractions for youth? Our young people need them more and more.

This is the challenge to you: incline your hearts towards the young people, in order that they may lift their hearts towards you! Be a blessing for the generation to come. Isn't that one of the reasons why God let you grow old?

16. "But I Can't Place the Name..."

He still looks fresh and fit. He is seventy-three years old, but he doesn't look his age when he is sitting there talking.

He speaks smoothly and with humor. Now and then he stops briefly: "Let me see, what was his name again? I can say it a hundred times but just now I can't think of it. Wait a moment ... no, pardon me, I just can't remember his name. Yes, that tells me that I'm getting old. It happens over and over these days that I lose track of names ... and oh, that's a nuisance."

Forgetting faces often goes hand in hand with forgetting names.

I once made the acquaintance of a new member of my congregation who was at an advanced age. For an hour we talked amicably. A week later I ran into him for a moment. "Who are you? I don't know you," was his first remark. He had completely forgotten my face and the talk we'd had.

How terribly unpleasant this sort of thing can be. It is possible that this condition will eventually result in our forgetting everything and remembering nothing. Medical science cannot do much for that as yet. The only weapon seems to be prayer.

I've had an aged couple in my parish who prayed daily: "Lord, please don't let us become senile."

Understandable, isn't it? Of course God does not answer every prayer of this type in the way we might wish. In any case, prayer is only a weapon against senility if that prayer is accompanied by work. What can be done?

Concerning faces, first of all, why do you forget them so soon? Because deep down these faces do not much interest you any longer. You have already seen so many faces. The first bear you saw you observed with great interest. When you move around in a zoo every day, bears hardly make an impression on you. So, too, it goes with seeing people in your old age. You should, therefore, observe new faces with great interest. You must try to retain a strong feeling of inquisitiveness about the life around you. After people who have visited you leave, try to recall their faces in your mind's eye. It takes a little more effort than it did once. But by exercising your attention you remain fit and sympathetic.

Concerning names, I suggest that you write down new names you learn. Repeat old ones. Keep a little notebook and study it from time to time.

A grandfather I know who has a multitude of grand-children and great-grandchildren is usually the first one to remember their birthdays with a postcard. He has not forgotten one of them yet, even though he is far past ninety. He has listed all these names and birthdays carefully on a calendar, and every day begins with a look at that list.

A lady of sixty, a minister's wife, still very active, found it a little irritating — maybe even sinful — that she couldn't remember on Monday what had been the sermon topic Sunday, even when she had entered into it vigorously when she heard it. She decided to write down the text, the theme, and the points of the sermon or the message and tape the note to the door of her kitchen cupboard. Each time she needed to be in the kitchen — and how often doesn't a woman at home have to — the note caught her eye and while she was busy doing her work reminded her of the message she had heard.

Wouldn't you be able to find a place for such a note? Wouldn't you be able to write down some remembered parts of the sermon when you've come home from church? Keep pen and paper handy when your memory becomes less reliable.

I also read of an old lady who was almost completely deaf and blind. Deafness and blindness practically shut one off completely from human life. One cannot read or hear. One could understand it if she had become self-centered and bitter. But the opposite was the case. This lady, in fact, was unusually friendly and good-humored. Why?

Mondays, she told me, are my history days. I find out how much I remember of biblical history. I put my whole self into it, and in that way I retain the events in my memory.

Tuesday is song day. I hum the songs I learned as a child. This gives me a delightful day.

Wednesday, it's catechism. I recite from the catechism whatever answers I can remember. This, too, is a fine day.

This lady knew how to make something good out of every day. And she exercised her memory, on which she now depended because no new impressions were entering through either eye or ear.

And then this loss of memory reminds us that we must let go of this life a little at a time. Let us attach our remembrances, then, more and more to the new world that is coming.

As the capacity to remember names decreases, the Christian has this comfort, that his memory goes to the place where *a new name* will be written on his forehead. And as he loses his ability to remember faces he has this comfort, that he goes with haste to that moment in which he sees God — whose he was and whom he served — face to face.

In addition he experiences that kind providence which makes a person able to retain his memory with respect to God and his cause the longest. I remember, for instance, a woman with whom no single contact seemed possible anymore. Her spirit was nearly completely quenched. Only when I recited a simple verse, such as "Safe in the arms of Jesus," did her eyes light up. At that moment she made contact and a glimpse of recognition occurred.

On deathbeds often only *one* name is mentioned and *one* face seen: *Jesus*. But then that is sufficient.

17. Moving

If you are at all acquainted with men and women in their early fifties, those who are approaching the portal of old age, you may have noticed that these people often struggle with the thought that they are going to remain until death in their present house or in their present job. To avoid that anxiety some of them go to great lengths to move or to change jobs, though they often regret such a change later.

For one who has passed the seventy-year mark, the cards often fall the opposite way. At that age one dreads any changes. Moving may be experienced as a disaster.

How difficult it often may be to remain living in a large house after the children have left. Younger people want plenty of room; older ones can't do the work in a large home anymore or find help to do it. Having someone live in is often worse than being in jail. In such a situation one is almost forced to look for smaller quarters.

Or your spouse has died, and you can no longer remain alone. You must break up housekeeping. You may end up living in with children. All these things you've grown used to you now must leave behind: your environment, your garden, your neighbors, your furniture, and so on.

Or, cutting in even deeper, you may become an invalid; the children cannot (or will not) accommodate you and you must go to a rest home.

Only the person who has experienced these things really knows what they mean. When you've grown old, moving is difficult. You don't feel at home elsewhere anymore. Old trees should not be transplanted.

I am thinking now of some visits and conversations that touch on those questions. Let me mention a few.

She lived in a small house: living room, bedroom, kitchen, and a small flower garden. She was 79, still rather alert, but her vision was growing dim and her hearing was beginning to fail. Sometimes she would not hear the doorbell.

"Shall I move in with the children? I believe they would like that. They've offered that I should do that at least once. What do you think, Pastor?"

"How old are *their* children?" I asked.

"Between fifteen and four — there are four of them."

"And how much space is available?"

"Well, with a lot of shifting and changing they may be able to have a small room open for me. But in the evening the oldest probably will have to do his homework there."

"Is there a garden?"

"No, it's a modern apartment building with a small balcony."

I told the lady without hesitation, "Don't do it. Don't do it as long as you can do without. If it does not work at all for you, we can see again. But if you do it now, you'll soon regret it."

She remained in her small house until her death.

I'd like to give that advice also to everyone who is growing older. Stay as long as possible in your own environment, in your own home or apartment. In that way you stay independent and you won't grow old too rapidly. And if it is absolutely impossible for you to stay where you are, submit yourself completely to that needed change. Don't be a know-it-all. Listen to advice from other people who mean well for you. Ask the opinion of your pastor or doctor.

A second conversation.

She had lived with her brother for many years. Suddenly he had died, and she could not stay alone in the house. So there she sat in her son's house. I was visiting her. Her mind was very alert. With an old-fashioned hearing aid, a horn, sitting close to me, she drank my words. That horn seemed like a cup that she filled each time with my words and then drank to the last drop.

"But now I've lost all my furniture," she told me. "It's at an auctioneer. Some of those pieces are very dear to me, especially my clock. I've kept that clock since my first marriage. You know that marriage only lasted for a few months. He died soon. I've got so many fond memories attached to that clock. It breaks my heart to see it go like that. I can't sleep at night because of it. Do you think I can get that clock back?"

I could see that this was no small matter to her. It was a piece of her life. What better thing could I do than drive to the auctioneer and pick up the clock before it could be auctioned off. Maybe it wouldn't have brought much money on sale, but to this lady the clock had far more value. This clock had regulated her life and her work year in and year out.

Don't get rid of all your furniture. Keep some pieces that remind of times past. . . .

A third conversation.

She is living with her son and daughter-in-law. There is no space for her to have her own room; and several of the grandchildren are teen-agers.

"Oh, Pastor! I'm sometimes so upset! What they're all doing here! My son allows it, but I can't understand it anymore. The children jeer and hoot at their parents and me. They come home late, bringing their friends with them, and they do whatever they wish. When I say something, I get backtalk. But I can't keep quiet for all that. What do you say about it?"

"Something that perhaps will surprise you," I replied. "Say as little as you can. When you are up against a real injustice, speak of it in a loving manner with your children and grandchildren. If it doesn't help, then leave the responsibility with them. Don't try to rear them. Meddle as little as possible."

"Oh, yes, you can give good advice," was the reply, "but you ought to have to sit in the middle of it, and you would be upset too."

Still I think people must meddle as little as possible in the household's rules for the children and in bringing them up. If you lived somewhere else, you'd not be involved. Now circumstances force you to be with them. You must handle things as neatly as when you lived fifty miles away. Your children are independent and should be allowed to take responsibility. Let it go with prayer and a warning.

A fourth conversation.

"I can't stand it here anymore. They just look at you and they remain complete strangers. My furniture, my house — if only I could have it all back. This is no life worth living!"

I heard this from someone who had only recently been admitted into a Christian rest home.

"You can get out if you want to," I said. "Just tell me where we should take you."

She didn't know. She couldn't go anywhere. None of her children offered her hospitality, and she could no longer be left alone.

"Then shouldn't you begin by being thankful that you're being looked after in this place? Think of what might happen to you if you weren't here."

She was silent.

"And also, what have you done yourself to make life more pleasant and bearable? Have you ever prayed for these people? Have you ever wondered how you could be a blessing in this place? Have you ever gone to the sick ward to make your acquaintance with the patients?"

She was still silent. Then she said, "Yes, that's how it really ought to be. But it's so terribly difficult. If you've had to let go of everything. . . ." She wept, and then we prayed together.

People who live in rest homes, make of living together what you can. Live in love for each other. Be a blessing. Don't just look at what is yours, but also at what befalls other people. In that way you can fulfil Christ's law of love.

Moving at an advanced age is a difficult assignment. It means letting go of things, leaving things behind. Moving of this kind brings to mind — and, as I see it, also prepares us for — the great move that awaits all of us: our leaving this earthly tent in order to move into the building which is not made with hands but is eternal in the heavens. We won't be able to take anything with us. "Funeral shirts have no pockets," the old saying goes. Have you already prepared yourself for this move?

When we move from one place to another on this earth, we often pack up small items well ahead of time. We take paintings off the walls. We prepare for our departure. Have you begun to make preparations for the great exodus? Or is everything still held together with strong glue? Is this life still everything to you?

"Prepared?" you may say. "Doesn't death come suddenly? I may live many more years. . . !"

Indeed. And yet. . . . Let me tell you what I mean by using a fable.

One day Death was in some sort of difficulty. On that day he happened to meet Mr. X.

"Please, help me," Death cried. "I'll reward you greatly."

Mr. X helped him. But Death could not promise that he would never come to get Mr. X. "I cannot make any exceptions," he said.

They agreed that the reward for Mr. X would consist of the promise that Death would warn him and give him ample notice before coming to get him.

After that day Mr. X lived on happily. He had no worries. When Death would come to give him notice, he would have more than enough time for repentance.

One day Death appeared.

"I've come to get you," he said.

"Come to get me?" Mr. X said, distressed. "But you were to warn me first!"

"But haven't I done so repeatedly?" Death answered.

"No, you haven't."

"Well, yes, I have. When you lost your first molar, wasn't that a warning? And when your hair turned grey and your eyesight became worse, and you turned deaf, and your breathing became more difficult; weren't all of these notices? So, no more talk of warnings: come with me, right now!"

You too have had warnings and repeated notices. Are you making preparations?

The great departure is near. Is there also a great yearning present?

18. Your Last Will

One of my colleagues told me how he had become involved in a property dispute. Farmer A claimed that Farmer B had moved the stone which marked the property line between their two parcels of land. They asked the minister if he would pass judgment in this quarrel, which had been going on for quite some time.

"Why do you ask *me* to pass judgment?" the minister inquired.

"To tell the truth," the answer came, "we ask you because it is much cheaper than hiring a lawyer."

I thought of this incident when I put down the title for this chapter. Perhaps you are hoping for some inexpensive advice from me about a last will and testament. Much to my regret I shall have to disappoint such expectations. But I hope that you will, nevertheless, read on.

I *am* talking about a testament.

I would like to tell you that you really should have your testament made up. Many people who are growing older still haven't done that. I can see you smiling:

"There isn't much to be made up in my case." Or, "Don't make me laugh, Pastor!" Fine. I'll get back to that in a while.

For many, however, there is another reason they haven't gotten round to making up a last will. They don't want to speak realistically about death and departure from this life, and they don't want to act soberly with that in mind.

I mentioned speaking and acting.

Older people do think of death, even though they can push these thoughts aside. Carl G. Jung, the Swiss psychologist, has said that thoughts of death increase in great number as one's age increases. One who grows older prepares himself, like it or not, for death.

Like it or not! An involuntary preparation for death often prevents a person from a realistic preparation.

Our times are conducive to pushing aside thoughts of death. In our cities death knells no longer toll. Cemeteries tend to be far removed from residential areas, and often look more like formal gardens than burial grounds. Dying people are taken out of the hospital ward and put into a private room. Some hospitals do not allow nursing personnel to speak about the patients who have died. Face-to-face encounters with death are limited to a minimum. In this way we are guided to speak as little about death as possible, and to consider dying.

In this respect our century is the exact opposite of earlier ones. Then there was a kind of death and cemetery cult. There was too much talk about death, too many tears too easily shed. Not death but life should motivate us. The Egyptians used to put a skull on the dinner table at mealtime. Emperor Maximilian carried a coffin along on all his expeditions. Another ruler, Wolfgang von Anholt, slept with a coffin next to his bed for fifteen years. We don't like such excesses. They're un-

Christian and exaggerated. But neither is it right to escape confrontation with death entirely.

"Set your house in order, for you must die," the Bible says (2 Kings 20:1). In the present situation this preparation does not have much of a chance. And I'm merely thinking now of the provisions for this life. Suddenly, when death comes, the survivors agonize about questions like "how would Mother have wanted that?" and "what should we do with this?" and "if he only had taken care of these things before."

In the Bible we meet two people who are thinking about saying farewell and dying, though they hardly mention these things to each other. I am talking about Elijah and Elisha. "And as they still went on, and talked . . . ," 2 Kings 2:11 states. There the two go together. Elijah knows he is making his last journey. Elisha, too, by divine revelation, knows that Elijah will be taken away from him.

But we get the impression that they talked about all kinds of things without naming concretely the one thing that filled their hearts and minds. The only word about Elijah's departure is this, "Ask what I shall do for you, before I am taken away from you." In other words, you can still ask me now, so you'd better do it. For a moment they touched on the great event: *before I am taken away from you.*

But even that little often goes unsaid among people who are close to each other. Please, talk these things over in detail with each other, before it is no longer possible. Ask your questions while you still can get an answer.

At least do not pretend that death does not exist. You, too, may be separated from each other any moment. There is an Oriental fable in which a strolling man was suddenly attacked by a tiger. He managed to escape by

91

jumping into a deep well. When he had nearly reached the bottom, he saw a dragon below lifting its head to catch him between its jaws. Terrified, the man grasped the thin stem of a plant that climbed up along the steep wall. With the courage of the desperate he climbed higher and higher, until he noticed that the tiger was still waiting for him at the edge of the well. There he hung between those wide open mouths, until he still noticed something else. Above his head a white mouse was gnawing the stem on which his life depended, and below his feet a black mouse was chewing. Any moment that stem could break off and the man would fall down and be torn to pieces.

In this story, the white mouse is the image of day and the black mouse represents night. Each day and each night gnaws a little piece off our lives. One moment, suddenly, the stem of life has been gnawed through entirely and then we die. It need not be a terrible disease or catastrophe that drags us down to the grave. Certainly, they lie in waiting, ready to pounce on us; but even when we escape this certain death, little mice are busy, meanwhile, unnoticed, to take us into the grave.

In view of this death that comes unexpectedly (a heart attack, a traffic accident, a stroke, cancer, and so many other things that may eventually break the thread of life) you must attend to setting matters in order.

You must speak calmly to your husband, your wife, your children, your friends about these things. You must speak about how things should go when you are no longer here. And so I return to those who say, "There's nothing for me to make a last will or testament about...." Perhaps so. Perhaps it doesn't seem to you to make sense to visit a lawyer or a notary public. But isn't it possible for you to make up a testament in a different sense? Shouldn't some things be discussed with your spouse, for instance, about what he or she should do when you are no longer at his or her side? Should he or she remain in the house in which you live? Should he or she ... but let me not mention all of the possibilities. If only you begin to talk about these things honestly and soberly, these several points will present themselves naturally.

Isn't there also something beautiful in writing, while you're alert and alive, some words of farewell to save in your desk drawer and eventually to be found by your survivors? If you have children, it seems to me a beautiful thought to bind something to their hearts, one after the other. Such a letter, when found among the documents, after your dying, will be read affectionately and always be treasured.

Disease may deteriorate your body in such a way that you do not find another opportunity to say or write anything of that type. I've stood at many a deathbed. Most people whom I saw dying died unconsciously. Deathbeds on which one can speak clearly and give an audible testimony aren't many — partly, perhaps, because pain-killing narcotic drugs are all too eagerly administered these days.

A dying person once told me: "I had wanted to write down a few things, something for the children, a sort of spiritual letter — but nothing came of it. Suddenly I was rushed to the hospital and you know the course of events. . . ." Our entire life must, of course, be a legible letter. But that does not take away the reality that such a written letter can become a valued treasure for those who are left behind.

In this connection let me speak a word of warning. Do not *bind* those who remain behind too much. It is best not to bind them to anything at all except the gospel. I mean this: there have been people have made their husbands or wives promise them before their departure that they should never remarry. Children have been forced to work in their parents' business. Similar promises have been extracted from other survivors. In this way burdens are laid on shoulders, burdens which in the course of time turn out to be unbearable.

You may not play the role of a prophet before your departure by determining for the future all sorts of things. Who can know what the future will bring? Perhaps the future will develop in such a way that all your plans and decisions will not fit within its framework and thus become dead weight. Moreover, promises extracted in this way bring serious conflicts of conscience to those who are left behind. I'm thinking of a man who had his son promise him to change nothing and not to expand his business. Bound in his conscience to this promise, the son did not dare make necessary adjustments later, when the times required changes. Consequently, the business went from bad to worse.

In any event, talk soberly, give advice, bind the survivors only to the word of the Lord, which always remains timely. Your talks and your ordering of things certainly do not have to be limited to the funeral arrangements. About these arrangements people do, from time to time, offer an opinion. I've known people who even wrote their own death announcement and the liturgy for their funeral. Be sober in these things and do not prescribe all sorts of details for your survivors. Watch for obvious pride, but also for hidden pride. Your name is not at stake.

An Egyptian sculptor, so the story goes, was commissioned to provide a stone column for the grave of one pharaoh. The highest column was to bear the name of the pharaoh. But the sculptor chiseled his own name into the stone. Then he used several layers of varnish to cover his own name, and in the hardened varnish he engraved the name of the pharaoh. He knew that in due time rain and wind would erode away this varnish and the name of the pharaoh; only his own name would stand the test of time. Be careful in your arrangements that you do not chisel your name in the stone hidden by the varnish. These arrangements are not for you, not to preserve your name, but for the benefit of those who are dear unto you and for the welfare of the kingdom of God. Hold fast what is good. "Owe no one anything, except to love one another" (Romans 13:8).

I should say something to people for whom it *does* make sense to see a notary public or a lawyer. One could of course go on at length about private property, about capital growth and real estate investments, about inheritance rights and annuities and tax shelters and the like. This is not the place for such discussions.

If, however, arrangements about property need to be made, have a will properly drawn and kept up to date with personal circumstances or desires. This *should* protect your right to convey property to your heirs in the manner you wish. But when you convey money or property, never forget that you are not a possessor but a steward: it is the Lord's.

If you have children, this will normally have consequences for your will. The Bible assumes that it is natural for parents to store up treasures for their children and not vice versa. Should there be difficulties in spite of that assumption (for instance, if you think that one should be cut out of the will), discuss them honestly and openly. Don't be secretive or mysterious about your last will and testament. And in any case, but particularly if your children are well off or live in comfortable circumstances, do not forget the needy or suffering causes in the Kingdom of God.

I am not about to make propaganda for one cause or another. But beware, lest arguing strangers attack your property soon after you are gone. So many a beautiful cause could be served with your resources. You have understood that I'm not sparing the cost of a notary public's or of a lawyer's services. These people cannot be substituted for. I'm only saying: do not put off till tomorrow what you can do today.

It will also give you peace of mind to know that you have made the best arrangements you were able to. Something of the confident resignation of "Now, Lord, let your servant depart in peace," comes over you when you've prepared your house in this fashion.

A well-prepared and updated will prevents difficulties, eases the farewell from this earth, wins time for the care of matters of the soul, and for showing thankfulness and forgiveness, and provides opportunities for the encouragement and upbuilding of many others to the glory of God.

I omitted one word that I would like to draw to your attention: *forgiveness.*

Is there anything that needs to be set straight? Then do it! Are there still quarrels, feuds? Reconcile these differences quickly.

At a deathbed I witnessed a reconciliation of a couple. Man and wife had not wanted to see each other for almost twenty years. At the edge of eternity the hands were again laid one in the other. But why not sooner?

A minister once visited a dying parishioner.

"Are you prepared to die?" he asked.

"Yes, thank God, I am," was the answer.

But the man had lived for years with feelings of hatred for another member of the parish. He had never been willing to attempt a reconciliation. Therefore, the minister asked, "Have you reconciled yourself with Brother X?"

"No."

"Will you do it now? May I go out and get him here?"

"Never, never!" the dying man cried.

"Then I must tell you that you are not prepared to enter the Kingdom of God, but you will remain outside," said the minister.

Hard to take. But yet it's true.

19. Homesickness

I have sometimes found among my older brothers and sisters a case of homesickness, a nostalgic longing for one's home, casting a longing, lingering look behind for the house in which one grew up, ruefully pining for his fatherland or his birthplace.

Homesick people are sick with longing for a former place in which they felt at home. Many of you have found it necessary to move and to adjust to new circumstances. Some know how to adapt easily to the new environment. But many no longer have the strength for that. They are filled with one thought; they want to return to the environment they were used to in the past. And because they know that this can never happen, a deep scar mars their souls. Some slowly pine away in homesickness.

I'm always very happy when this sickness does not get hold of a person in his days of growing older, because there's hardly a medicine known for this ailment. Some people, aware of the truth that "you can't go home again," take things in their own hands and end their life by suicide.

But I would rather not talk further about this homesickness. I would prefer to draw your attention to another kind of homesickness which I do not find often enough. I'm talking about the longing for heaven, for the new earth, for God. In contrast to the usual kind of homesickness, this kind of sentiment could be called a yearning for, a longing toward, a place, a home, in the future.

A minister once wrote to his congregation:

When I visit aged people, I am struck time and again by the small degree of longing to depart and be with Christ. Even when these persons are well over eighty, even though their marriage partner has died, even though they become more lonesome each day, they still like to linger in this world. In the event of illness they long yet to be restored to health. They do not struggle or fight back when God comes to take them home, but the Father's House does not evoke any positive feeling of homesickness, either. Occasionally I meet someone who strongly desires to depart, but more often this desire is not felt among the aged. I am very concerned about this.

I believe that this minister's picture is realistic.

Certainly, some aged persons do have hearts that burn for what is to come. "Let me come to you, Lord," they pray. "Why must I wait still longer?" When a physician wanted to give one of my old, sick-to-death members of the congregation an injection because the life-elixir was visibly diminishing, she said, "Please, doctor, no. Why should we bother with that; I'm going to Jesus, and if you give me another injection, I must wait yet longer."

But I also remember the statement of the unbelieving doctor we quoted earlier: "I don't believe there are any real Christians, because none of them wants to die."

This is a strong statement and a little exaggerated, it seems to me. But undoubtedly the general impression gained in his medical practice must have caused him to say such a harsh thing.

I am aware that in old age diminishing psychological strength plays a role. One who grows older does not act or react as intensely as he did when he was younger. Hate and love taper off and become weaker, because the human spirit diminishes and grows weaker. I once heard an older, devout brother say, "Pastor, it is often difficult for me to accept that even in church many things just pass me by, even these things that used to touch me deeply. Often these things now barely affect me." Thus decreased strength may be a factor affecting the degree of our involvement.

But shouldn't one's interest in heavenly things be stronger than in the things that pass? Among many I do not find that to be the case. Thus, this sad phenomenon, this not longing for heaven, cannot be explained away in terms of factors of diminishing strength.

What, then, is the cause?

Among children one finds a longing for heaven often much stronger than among old people. When the sunset paints a golden gate in the sky, a child would like to walk out there and go through the gate. I remember this from my own childhood. When a child sees a beautiful, sun-drenched cloud floating by, he expects that Jesus will appear on that cloud any moment. When a young child once was reproached for being careless in crossing the street, "Child, you could have been killed!", he answered, "What does it matter? When you die you go to heaven, don't you?" Pointing at a beautiful star-filled sky during an evening walk, another child said, "Dad, if the wrong side of heaven is that beautiful, how splendid the good side must be!"

Have you, old brother and sister, lost that first love and that childlike faith during your long life? Is it possible that you don't long so intensely for heaven any more, because deep down in your heart you don't believe in heaven so strongly anymore?

If this is the case, read this line from Psalm 42 over and over:

> Why are you cast down, O my soul,
>> and why are you disquieted within me?
> Hope in God; for I shall again praise him,
>> my help and my God.

I can imagine that persons who do not share the faith that after this life the real life will come hold on with tightened grip to the things of this life. Thoughts of death bring new life to one's life, don't they? We appreciate anew, or for the first time, the things we will have to do without when we die. The value of life is intensified in the face of death. We are like children who do not want to go to bed at night and suddenly discover the toys they want to play with.

But when glory awaits us, must we still act like children who delay getting ready for bed in every way they can? Understand me correctly; I'm not about to say that at your old age you should become unfaithful to earth. By saying this I would erase everything I've said in the preceding conversations. I'll still say: as long as you live, God has a task for you! While you're alive you *must* occupy yourself with the things of this world.

In the middle of his work, which made him aware that it would be more beneficial for the church if he would remain alive, St. Paul *longed* to depart to be with Christ. Can things be quite right with you if such a longing is barely found within you, even though your task has grown so small that you sometimes wonder: why am I still here?

Is it not just then when that beautiful old song by Van Alphen should come to your mind:

> As I draw nearer
> to the house of my Father,
> I yearn more and more
> for the heavenly mansion,
> where after life's battle
> my King's blessing awaits.

I believe that the reason we live so little in hope is that we haven't thought enough of the *glory* that awaits us.

Once I found a widow in tears. Understandably so: her husband had died and he had been a wonderful marriage partner. But when she cried, "But he got to enjoy his pension for such a brief period," I was strangely surprised for a moment. What's a good pension compared to a heaven full of bliss? Who would pity himself about losing a dime if he gained a million dollars?

"I consider (not only) that the *sufferings* of this present time are not worth comparing with the glory that is to be revealed unto us" (Romans 8), but also that the *glory* of this age is no match for the glory that is to be revealed unto us.

If the gates are of gold, what will the halls be like when I enter? Don't we linger too much in the portals? Don't we peek often enough through the openings in the gate at the halls filled with glory?

To borrow, once more, from another minister:

I too have sometimes come under the charms of that quiet life turned inward. When you sit next to an old mother on a dark wintry day — a cozy little room, hearth burning wood, teapot above a wax candle-flame, old-fashioned clock ticking peacefully — and you hear how pleasantly and quietly she lives . . . , yes, when you see these things and absorb the peace, you think sometimes: isn't that just right? Isn't the inner life really what counts?

An old house in Holland bears this inscription: "In this place may I evade the thunder claps of the world." Isn't it pleasant to stand alongside the road, watching life without having to join in the current? At such a time we don't mind God's call, "Wouldn't you rather come home, my child?" But usually we do not experience an intense longing for God's call to come home.

Later in our conversations we will talk about the glory that awaits us. But now I'll say in advance, Think much more often, and much more concretely, about that glory: visualize it, envision it. Compared to that glory the luster of the earthly is but a faint shadow. Remember that the form and appearance of this world will pass. You may see something of that passing away and that going downhill in your own life. So much more you are reminded to lift up your heart.

God's children should sing this hymn as they draw nearer:

> The mention of thy glory
> Is unction to the breast,
> And medicine in sickness,
> and love, and life, and rest.
>
> O one, O only mansion!
> O Paradise of joy!

103

Where tears are ever banished
        And smiles have no alloy;
Thy loveliness oppresses
        All human thought and heart,
And none, O Peace, O Zion,
        Can sing thee as thou art.

O sweet and blessed country,
        The home of God's elect!
O sweet and blessed country
        That eager hearts expect!
Jesus, in mercy bring us
        To that dear land of rest,
Who art, with God the Father,
        And Spirit, ever blest.
                    Amen.
— *St. Bernard of Cluny, ca. 1145*

If only I knew where I'll be then. . . . If only I could be sure of my salvation. Many people respond to this conversation with remarks like that. I won't say much about that, just ask a few questions.

Is this the only answer of your old age to the faithful care God has shown you year in and year out? Listen to what he says in Isaiah 46:4:

Even to your old age I am He,
        and to grey hairs I will carry you.
I have made, and I will bear;
        I will carry and will save.

Do you have a right to say in reply to this, "I don't know if this is meant for *me?*" Would God be a liar? Can't you trust him? Don't you by saying such things pass the blame on to God?

Pray, therefore, for the Holy Spirit. (And wouldn't God give his Spirit to one who asked him for it?) When

104

God sends his Spirit, eyes are opened and people will see from afar the city that has foundations, whose architect and builder is God.

One who has received God's Spirit as firstfruit looks forward, stretches himself toward the revelation of the children of God!

A final word. Do not long superficially for what is forthcoming. I meet aged persons whose life's evening (in the earthly sense) is very somber and cheerless. They remind me of Job. One bad experience after another befalls them, and everything is being taken away from them. These people then say: "I wish I could get off here. God had better take me away. I have nothing left here. Lord, please bring my life to an end now."

A Christian who lives from the promises in the Bible, immediately knows that these experiences may not be a motive for wanting to depart from this life. He may wish that the tears will be wiped away, but if that's the only reason why he would want to go to heaven, he will be disillusioned — not by God, but by himself.

Only the one who has cleansed his clothing, that is, his life, in the sacrificial blood of Christ, and who yearns to serve him faultlessly, is able to appear before God without fear. A desire to escape from this life because of misery and adversity need not be related to that longing for service in perfection.

A dry leaf falls down in front of my window — an early messenger of approaching autumn. The leaf reminds me of a minister I knew, who used to draw thousands of hearers around his pulpit. One day such a leaf fell on his window sill. He took it to be a letter of death addressed to him. In a poem, long forgotten, he wrote down his feelings about this. The verse may not be great literature, but it's worth reading.

Death has written me a letter;
I read it on a yellowed leaf
That, driven onward by a stormwind,
Had settled on the window sill.
I read, "Wanderer, speed your step.
The evening falls, the night descends.
Do what you can, do it today,
Tomorrow may not find you here.
Willingly carry what you must bear,
Soon your cross falls from your shoulder,
Awaits through God's eternal goodness,
Your crown at the other side of the grave!"

And I wrote back, "Thank you, feared King,
For letting me, your weary subject,
Upon approaching, calmly to glance ahead
At his eternal, final home.
I hear the rustling of your feet,
But I do not fear your face;
As liberator I may greet you,
Who offers me rest for unrest.
Now free this heart and dim my senses,
Quench if you must the last light of my life;
Yet, conquered, I shall conquer with you,
And death — where is your victory?"

What do you write back?

20. Unexpected Visitors

I rang the doorbell at the home of an aged couple.

The window drapes moved slightly for an instant. A searching look on the face of a woman discovered me on the doorstep. I noticed a slight expression of alarm on her face when she saw me.

As the drapes remained hanging to one side without her noticing it, I was allowed a view into the room. I saw the cause of her alarm. The room was somewhat disorderly. With great speed, the woman nervously tried to set things straight before opening the door. Upon her cry, "The minister!", her husband jumped up from his chair. As quickly as he could he put on his shoes and his suit coat.

I watched all this going on through the window. Then the door opened.

"Pastor, please come in; how nice that you could come by again...."

A moment later I am led into a neat and orderly room.

"Well, I must say, you've managed to put things straight very quickly, people!" I said naughtily.

They felt discovered. Together we laughed and joked some more about what had happened.

The text, "Behold, the Judge is standing at the doors" (James 5:9), tells you that the *Lord* may enter anytime. For the world at large this word points to the day of judgment; for you personally it means your last breath. Then you must appear before him. Then he appears before you.

This appearance will take place unexpectedly.

That visit, too, comes at a time when you least expect it and find yourself amidst disorderliness, literally and figuratively.

A minister whom I used to hear preaching became seriously ill. When he recovered he said, "God has rung my doorbell."

Are you prepared for him to ring your doorbell for a last visit? Does anything need setting straight? Are there any hidden idols, such as Rachel had, which need to be removed from your life? Do you have any making up to do? Are things between you and God, between you and your wife, your children, your neighbor . . . in order?

Will you let him in?

Look, he stands at the door. He may ring the doorbell any moment.

When I filled an out-of-town preaching engagement, I was led into the guest room by my host on Saturday night. After he had left, I looked around me curiously: in what environment would I be spending this night? Suddenly I noticed a large poster hanging above the bed. The poster read: "Can you die the way you're living now?"

Whatever went through my mind at that moment, it certainly was not this. That's why that question struck me so strongly. I thought quietly about that question for a moment and then answered. Now I'm passing this question on to you.

"Can you die the way you're living now?"

Soon your doorbell may ring. He, the judge, will stand on the doorstep of the house of your life.

IN THE DOOR

21. Left Alone?

To this point we have been imagining ourselves sitting down together near the window, or near the fireplace, to talk. But with someone who is dying a long conversation is no longer possible. He lets go of us. He stands as it were with one foot in another world where we have never been, and at any moment he may pull the other foot over as well. Maybe he will lift up his head once more to say something, to ask something. . . . Maybe he will open his eyes for one more brief look with an expression we will never forget. But calm, extended conversation has become impossible. Those standing around the bed watch their footsteps and muffle their voices.

The dying person has arrived at what has been called a borderline situation, and at that point we can no longer follow him. We lose him and he loses us.

So we cannot continue to talk when you are standing inside the gate of death and I am standing outside. We can only converse together — perhaps "stammer" is a better word — about being in that door to eternity while both of us are still standing outside it.

That conversation will be very modest. No one can speak from experience about being in the gate, not even those who have stood on the edge of eternity and barely escaped death. They have not actually experienced death. It has been said that a psychology of dying is impossible to write. We shall not try to do that here either. Let us only speak and think of what we have heard and seen at deathbeds and of what we have read about dying in the Bible.

One thing is certain: one who enters the door to eternity must let go of everything and enter into extreme loneliness. No matter how lovely people have been, no matter how costly their possessions, one must leave them all behind.

In a sense, one who is dying *wants* to be left alone. Think, for example, of Elijah and Elisha. Both know that Elijah's end has come. Elijah seeks solitude. He wants to be alone when that strange thing happens to him. He bids farewell to the schools of the prophets and he tries to dissociate himself from his faithful co-worker Elisha.

"Remain here," he says repeatedly to Elisha. "For the Lord has sent me to Gilgal, to Bethel." His wish to be left alone clearly comes through in these words. One must wrestle through that narrow gate alone. No human being can ultimately assist you in going through. For that reason many will be left alone in those moments.

But Elisha, for his part, cannot leave his great master alone. He wants to remain with him till the end and assist him if he can. He is not put off that easily. "As the Lord lives, and as you yourself live, I will not leave you," he says.

And so they keep on walking together. A difficult situation. We can understand the desire of each of them. The story shows us, however, that we should not impose ourselves on dying people. In any case, we ought not, as I have often seen, to stand in a semi-circle around a deathbed, certainly not while the minister is paying the dying person his last visits. Often relatives come around from all corners of the house to hear the dying person say something special. But by doing so they spoil completely the atmosphere for such a last, deep encounter. Wouldn't you rather retreat modestly? Perhaps the dying one still has a confession to make or something to say which he would not feel free to say in the presence of others.

I also have witnessed dying persons who could not die because they were prevented from dying by the on-lookers. Dying is an act between God and man alone. At best, the most intimate family is admitted to witness that event. And I have seen a dying person request even those family members to leave in order to be alone. I'm thinking of an old brother who loved his wife very deeply. They already had said farewell a few times and each time they sat together again, waiting for the end. "You had better leave the room now, dear," he said finally. When she had just left, he died.

Death leads us — in whatever way — into desolation and loneliness, and separates us. The book *The Great Hall,* which we have mentioned several times, portrays this last, lonesome struggle in a very penetrating manner. As you recall, the author describes the dying of an old woman who has one daughter and no one else in the world. She has spent her last days tired and lethargic in a rest home. In this home is a large hall. Whenever one of the residents becomes ill or deteriorates so much that the end may be expected, he is transferred to that hall. The touching part of the book is its portrait of a group of extinguished lives that, as they kibitz and banter together, have only one last prospect — that great hall.

115

The old woman, who is one of the wisest in the home and who always has felt like a stranger there, becomes ill and lies dying in the great hall. Her daughter Helen has come from Paris and is standing at the bedside. Even though life did not offer this old lady anything to cling to, she nonetheless looked fearfully and apprehensively into that great hall. Whenever someone was carried into that hall and died, she thought, "One day I shall be lying there like this woman. Alone. Shall I be alone in that last hour? No — Helen will certainly come. I'll hold her hand. Maybe I won't even notice it when I have to take that big step."

Before Helen arrives, one hears her sigh, "I'm so afraid. Anxiety presses like a heavy burden upon my chest and I can hardly swallow. If only you were here.... But if you were here, could you really help me? Or ... or ... what is it again Helen said once? 'Man is so terribly lonesome, my dear mother.' "

Later the old lady sighs again, "Anxiety, that choking anxiety is back again. One indivisible moment I was inside the black tunnel of which I could not see the end. With my remaining strength I could barely escape that terror of the unknown. This has been my last time. I know it. The moment is coming inescapably when I'll have to go through that tunnel.... I must go through it to the end. What may be there? What's at the end? I was afraid. Is there nothing left that can help me? No. I am alone. No man can still do something for me. God! Help me!"

But when Helen comes, the woman barely recognizes her. Bits of conversation follow.

"I've come immediately," said Helen.

"Yes," said the mother, "I knew it. I was waiting for you. I already was in front of the black tunnel that

I must go through alone. I'm so afraid. What is at the end?"

Shortly thereafter the mother loses consciousness. Her hands restlessly move from the heart to the throat and from the throat to the heart. The narrative says: "I took her hands in mine. They were ice cold. But I could not hold them. This struggle, her last one, she had to fight alone. . . ."

This description is so profoundly true, so deeply moving through its soberness and genuineness. Dying is entering into the ultimate loneliness.

As we said earlier, the author does not offer any Christian hope in this book. She does not show the great comfort in life and death. How richly and joyfully that comfort lights up over against the drab loneliness of this dying one without God. When everything caves in and all loved ones fall away, a poet may say:

> I may yet find refuge with you,
> but how shall it be in that night
> when winds howl like wolves
> and that eternal court of justice awaits us?

At that time, for the Christian, Jesus is there. The Bible says, ". . . and they saw no one, but Jesus alone." That's how it will be in the hour of death for the children of God.

> Though death may close the curtain of this life,
> Your cross, dear Lord, stands on your farthest shores.
> We grasp, still comforted, your outstretched hands,
> And know we're born again into your light.

He who took death and sin upon himself has promised the believer, "I *am* with you, always. . . ."

"Even though I walk through the valley of the shadow of death, Thou art with me...."

> My faith holds His hand firmly,
> Till my last few moments;
> And no power of death or grave,
> Ever pulls me away from Jesus!

Christ Jesus puts an end to the loneliness of the dying one. He is the guide when his children make that last journey. He will accompany us even into death. After hearing the story of *The Great Hall*, with its final hopelessness, one should read Romans 8, with its jubilant comfort. *"Nothing* can separate me from the love of God in Christ Jesus: *neither death,* nor life."

Do you dare to undertake that last journey alone? Will you go through that dark tunnel in solitude? Let me warn you: the burden will be too heavy for you. Go to your mediator. Let the only one who can give you strength accompany you. Remain faithful to the Lord of glory. He will not forsake you.

22. The Mystery

In his book *Bambi* author Felix Salten has two autumn leaves that remained on a tree branch engage in conversation.

"What will happen to us when we fall off?" one asks.

"We go down," answers the other.

"How is it there?"

"I don't know. One says one thing, another says something else, but no one knows. No one who once was down has ever come back to talk about it."

We ask the same question: what will happen to us when we die? Throughout the ages people have thought about that question. In a large mausoleum in the Netherlands there stands before the *columbarium* — the place where the urns containing the ashes of cremated bodies are kept — a sculpture of a female figure, hand above the eyes, contemplatively staring into the distance. The statue portrays our continuous thinking on the mystery of death.

One who follows that thinking on death soon discovers that views of life and the world are intimately connected with concepts of death. Each concept of death contains a view of life.

In this book we cannot discuss all these views or concepts at length. I would merely like to share several comments. The diverse views of life and death are clearly distinguishable into two groups — one optimistic, the other pessimistic.

Among optimistic views (even though, in my opinion, there is not a single bit of joy or glory in this idea) is included the way materialists understand death: as the decomposition of a certain physical composite. As that body decomposes, what we understand as consciousness, spirit, and soul disintegrate as well. Death ends all. Therefore, it is said, don't worry. This is the normal order of things; it's a natural phenomenon. If anyone still has difficulty with the fact of death, he may be comforted by a remark of the philosopher Epictetus, "When death comes, you are no longer here; and when you are here, death has not yet come. Therefore, remain calm." This same man once said that no one needs to be afraid of death, because death really is nothing but a mask grinning at you. "Turn the mask around and you will find that it does not bite." Epictetus concludes that the greatest disaster in your life is not death, but fear of death.

In a similar vein is the inscription once seen on the gate of a cemetery: "Make life good and beautiful; there is no hereafter, no meeting again." Some people say that you should banish all thought of death from your life; that you should live as though death does not exist. Others say, No, you should think often of death, you should face death courageously. That soul is worthy of admiration, it is said, which is prepared to separate itself from the body at any time.

120

Another optimistic view holds that at death one is assimilated into a total, universal form. As salt dissolves in water, as a drop of water is absorbed by the ocean, so the individual disappears and the universal emerges. Some also maintain that they continue to live in a different form or state of being. The famous German poet Goethe wrote, at the age of seventy-five:

> When a man has become seventy-five years old, he cannot help thinking of death at times. But let that thought rest entirely, because I am firmly convinced that our spirit is of a nature that is absolutely indestructible; that spirit operates from eternity to eternity. It resembles the sun that only seems to go under through our earthly eyes, but that in reality never goes under, but unceasingly continues to give light.

Goethe also thought that nature was obliged to give a new way of existence, if the present one would no longer do, to such a hard worker as he was.

Those who view the body as a limitation of the human spirit, to whom the spirit is a divine spark that is set on fire at death, are very optimistic about death. In their thinking, this human spirit reunites with the Divine Being in death. This ancient view is already found in Plato's dialogue *Phaedo,* and occurs repeatedly in Oriental religions.

But above these optimistic sounds one always hears pessimistic ones. These pessimistic sounds grow stronger the more mankind is beset by wars and disasters. Poets have always written poignantly out of such a view of death. Marsman, for example, makes the point directly:

> I am afraid of the hour
> in which death will unbind my body
> and my spirit will be put into the fire.

121

Another poet, Achilles Mussche, complains in "O Death":

> How shall I stand before you at the end of my life
> when I, lost beyond rescue in my need,
> come to surrender to you with a last gasp,
> pleading, it is enough, this darkness is too much?
>
> How shall I stand, staring from your thin edges,
> given up by all and distant to all things,
> a man who has nothing left but his two empty hands,
> who waits for the waving of the last of shooting stars?

Man today knows himself attacked by death. It used to be easier to banish death from our thoughts or to dress it up like a gentleman. But for many contemporary thinkers death is the governing principle of life and thought, existence is actually one large chunk of death.

Outside of the Christian faith, thoughts about dying oscillate between optimism and pessimism, from one extreme to the other. These thoughts are accompanied by similar attitudes toward death, which may range from indifference to it to longing for it.

In his famous sculpture "The Burghers of Calais," Rodin has portrayed six different attitudes man assumes in the presence of that "king of terrors." Six citizens, dressed in robes of penance, with a rope around the neck, had been surrendered to the enemy. Their dying would liberate the city. One old man is walking without fear. He bows his head in acceptance of his lot. He wants to be a wise man. Next to him goes someone who carries the keys of the city. He is not quite as old as the first one. He still may expect something from life, but by the power of his will he has overcome the revolt of his heart against his terrible fate. This man is about to sacrifice himself. Then comes a strong, young man, who walks toward his death, full of energy.

But next to these men, three other persons move along with drooping shoulders and shivering bodies. One is a boy who, questioning fearfully, says farewell to life. Another is a man who grasps his head in his hands in confusion and wonders painfully what is really taking place here. Finally, one sees a man whose trembling legs have given out; he has fallen prey to despair.

Perhaps you wonder how Christian theologians and philosophers have spoken of death. The answers to that question could fill a book. Most often dying is understood as the separation between soul and body. The spirit, the soul, returns to God and the body returns to the earth, where it remains until the day of resurrection. At that time body and soul will be reunited.

In our day the body is appreciated much more than previously. Psychologists and philosophers, Christians among them, are beginning to view man much more as a unity, in which the soul is not the greater nor the body the lesser. Consequently, some no longer approve of talking about a divided body and soul. The total human being dies, so it is said, and one day shall be resurrected. In that view also there is no intermediate state between death and the final resurrection, during which the spirit or soul is with God. According to other thinkers, the person after death but before the resurrection remains in existence only in the mind of God. Again, other Christians hold that all of man dies; but the heart, which is the element in man which stands beyond time, is lifted up to God.

Opinions differ considerably, don't you think? This should not be surprising, because dying remains a mystery. The Bible does not state *exactly* what happens to the human being at death. What I mean is that it does not provide any kind of anthropology or psychology of dying. I do think, however, that the old concept of the separation of body and soul (one may substitute "heart" or "spirit" for soul, I think) may present best what God's Word has to say in different places about dying. I read that Jesus, for instance, when he died, gave up the spirit to the Father and that afterwards his body was buried. This also confirms what is described at the end of the Book of Ecclesiastes and in other scriptural references. Also, the intermediate state, taught by the Scriptures, need not be pushed aside in this view.

Scripture, however, does not concern itself very much with the question of what happens, physically and humanly speaking, at death. Concerning death the Bible stresses three other things much more: (1) death is inescapable; (2) death is a form of punishment; and (3) death puts us under the judgment of God. The *religious* aspect of death receives all the emphasis; the other questions of what actually happens are merely incidental.

1. *Death is inescapable.* This is a thought to which everyone, like it or not, must agree. When the Bible asks, "What man can live and never see death? Who can deliver his soul from the power of Sheol?", no one can arise and call out, "I can!"

Not you, either.

James calls persons who are continuously devising schemes and making plans arrogant boasters — as if they were going to live forever: "Come on now, you who say, 'Today or tomorrow we will go into such and such a town and spend a year there and trade and get gain'; whereas you do not know about tomorrow. What is your life? For you are a mist that appears for a little time and then vanishes. Instead you ought to say, 'If the Lord wills, we shall live and we shall do this or that.' As it is, you boast in your arrogance" (James 4:13-16).

Yes, we often live and talk as though there were never an end to life. But when I look out over a congregation, I can say, "In a hundred years not one of these people will still be alive!" And the same goes for a beach full of sun-tanned people enjoying their relaxation. The baby eagerly nursing at its mother's breast, that precious bundle of new life, will die after a period of time. "Wherever we walk, a skeleton is with us," the saying goes.

In his book, *The Course of Death,* Corçao says: "That man who does not think goes to the movies three times a week. He borrows a little of the greatness of the filmstrip. He is a hero with the hero, infatuated with the lover, courageous with the strong. After his heroes ride into the sunset, he returns home, armed with death. Why, why?"

Death is powerful. And inescapable.

2. *Death is a punishment.* The Bible is the one book that makes the connection between death and sin and guilt. Only Christianity knows of mortality as a witness and evidence of sin. One does not find that connection in other religions.

Death has crept into man's world through sin. And this sin was rebellion against God, a falling away from God, who is the source of life.

3. *Dying puts us under the judgment of the heavenly judge.*

"I tell you, on the day of judgment men will render account for every careless word they utter," says Jesus (Matthew 12:36).

"It is appointed for men to die once, and after that comes judgment" (Hebrews 9:27).

125

"For we must all appear before the judgment seat of Christ . . ." (2 Corinthians 5:10).

Death may be a mystery, but these three things are clear. They cannot lead to misunderstanding. For that reason the Bible places these three thoughts in the brightest light.

When we have thought about these things in that light, it does not come as a surprise that the Christian really does not always have an easy time of dying. Thoughts of his sins and of the forthcoming judgment may overcome him. In contrast to the struggling, dying Christian, people who hold to one of the theories mentioned above may sometimes die more calmly.

But yet Christians frequently die with jubilation, because the Bible also mentions a fourth thought. That thought is central, particularly in the New Testament: Christ has come to take away sin and to conquer the power of death, thus bringing salvation from the judgment to come. Through his victory, the great turning point in the life of men can be moved from death to life. The decisive moment is no longer dying but being transformed from one's spiritual death into Life, being implanted by faith in Christ, being crucified with him, so that reborn we may arise and follow him into Life. The great, decisive turning point falls in the center of our lives. As a Christian saying has it: "One who dies before he dies, does not die when he dies."

And so a Christian who firmly believes that all has been finished for him may go quietly — yes, triumphantly — into death. The one person may be more discomfited by his own nervous character or by attacks of the evil one or by doubt than another. But may our hearts remain firm in the Lord even in the greatest vexation. In the deepest sense of the word a "struggle for death," then, is no more. That struggle took place, in all its height and depth and breadth, on Golgotha, and as a minor after-struggle in the hour of conversion.

> When I die, I die no more,
> Life smiles at me from afar,
> A life hard-won by Jesus.
> Whenever he bids me to come,
> I go. I do not fear the move,
> For I shall be safely with him.

We shall now notice briefly the description Paul gives of the act of dying in 2 Corinthians 5.

"We *know*," Paul says. He speaks from certainty, and all believers with him share that.

What is it that we know with certainty? We know that, when "the earthly tent we live in is destroyed," there is a palace for us with God. To a Christian, dying is transferring from the tent into the palace. Moving.

Once I visited an eight-sided hall of mirrors. First, we saw ourselves multiplied by thousands, or so it seemed. Then suddenly all was dark. The floor underneath our feet was turning. The props on stage were changed, accompanied by much noise. Children clung in fright to their parents, and for a moment even the adults wondered what was happening. Then the light was turned on again, and we were surrounded by beautiful woods with warbling birds and countless colors.

At that moment I could not help thinking of death. One moment everything will become dark. The stage is being changed, radically transformed. Only the enlightening appearance of Jesus will be with us in that darkness. And then, suddenly, heaven, eternal bliss, joy that never fades.

Paul adds as the only condition for moving to the

heavenly mansion that "by putting it on, we may not be found naked," but clothed. By that he means that the only condition for entering life at death is that we are covered by Christ's holiness and justice.

Then, really, in its deepest meaning death is no longer difficult. Not because we are looking at death through rose-colored glasses or have made it into a sort of kindly gentleman, not because we have intoxicated ourselves a little with alcohol and cannot see things clearly, not because we put our heads in the sand and no longer want to see, but because Christ has pulled the teeth from death, and has downgraded it to an usher for me, his child. Death opens the door for me to eternal life. And so dying is no longer a payment for sin, but a dying away of sin and a thoroughfare to eternal life.

Death, where is your sting?

23. Why?

To one who is in Christ many beautiful things can be said about dying. Yet I am often asked by elderly people, why is death still necessary for the Christian? Why can't Christians just enter heaven without that miserable grave?

This question even found a place in the Heidelberg Catechism: "Since Christ died for us, why do we still have to die?" (Q. 42). Dying is accompanied by many why's. *"Why* that husband and father, or that wife and mother, but not that senile old grandfather?" *"Why* this brother who means so much and not that blasphemer?" *"Why* is my husband being taken away now when I need him more than ever?"

Added to all these questions is the why about dying itself. Hasn't Christ died for us? Isn't everything finished? Hasn't heaven been opened to all who are in Christ Jesus?

Then why still that despicable experience of death? Why those frightful funerals? Why must the body of the beloved one whom you have cherished deteriorate so that you cannot stand the sight or touch of it anymore? Isn't then Christ a complete savior after all?

Why? Why?

What can I say to this? Let's not suppose that we can iron out all the pleats in our emotions and thoughts regarding these things. In this respect, too, we know only in part. Our answer, then, can be only a partial one.

Try to reverse things in your mind. Suppose that true Christians did not in fact die like non-Christians. Instead, like butterflies a beautiful new form would suddenly break forth from an inconspicuous cocoon. Imagine that you and I, having grown old and shriveled up, were suddenly to arise like angels with one impressive wingstroke.

Or, if you find that image too difficult, suppose that one good day angels were to come flying into the windows of Christians to carry them off on their wings. Or if you prefer an even more common way of putting it, imagine that we Christians did not grow older, never became ill, and always continued to live fresh and vigorous lives.

Imagine this concretely. You are standing at the grave of an unbelieving neighbor, a jovial man, a fine father, but not a Christian. The casket is lowered. All those present are weeping. Suddenly, an angel works his way through the crowd, reaches out his hand to you, allows you to say goodbye quietly, and then takes you away, heavenbound.

What if things really happened that way? Wouldn't the servant be glorified publicly before and above the Master? We *see* Jesus crowned with glory and honor, says the Letter to the Hebrews (2:9). *We* see; unbelievers see nothing of it; rather, they see the contrary. The seeing now is by *faith*. One day all eyes shall see him when he returns on the clouds of heaven, when he is glorified publicly. Even those who pierced him will behold him.

But we still await that appearance in glory. That day remains unrevealed. Would it be fitting for us to become visible publicly as victors and glorified people at a time when the great Master has not as yet become visible in glory and honor?

May the servants in the house raise their glasses and begin celebrating while the Lord and Master is still making preparations for the feast? The writer of the Letter to the Hebrews says in the same breath, "As it is, we do not see everything in subjection to him." The only one we now see, *by faith,* is Jesus, crowned with glory and honor. We do not see that as yet in man.

And that is why we still die just like those who do not have that faith. That is why we are buried and decompose just like these other people.

The servant does not rank above his master. The servant follows his master. This, I think, is the most important answer to the question of why we must still die.

But there is more to be said. Would we be able to enter heaven just as we are, without a radical change?

Would our bodies as they are now fit into that environment? In the Old Testament no Levite who had any physical defect was allowed to serve in the earthly temple. Would any defects be allowed in that true and heavenly tabernacle? Would that be permissible in the abode where the ultimate beauty himself reigns? The mortal body must undergo a complete revision, if I may put it that way. More is needed than a repair job, more than a new patch on an old garment. The body must be completely restored and transformed. It is death which must effect that great change. It is the narrow gate we must go through in which we have to drop quite a few things. It is the *thoroughfare* to eternal life, and it is, according to Jesus' word, narrow.

In the new world we shall no longer marry nor eat and drink as we do now. How would our present body, dependent on food and drink, be able to function there? That body must die, in order to be totally rebuilt. A natural body is sown, and a spiritual body will be resurrected.

The reason this does not take place in one indivisible split-second, as it will on the day of his coming, is because Christ has not yet been glorified visibly. Even on Easter morning his enemies did not see him, though the disciples did. But on the day of judgment he will have been glorified visibly, and bodies will be able to be completely rebuilt in a fraction of a second, from earthly to heavenly, from mortal to immortal. But not now.

And what of the spiritual part of my existence: may I enter into heaven as I am? May you?

Who would dare to say yes, after listening to the words written in Revelation 21: "But nothing unclean shall enter it, nor anyone who practices abomination or falsehood, but only those who are written in the Lamb's book of life." And in the next chapter, "Outside are the dogs and sorcerers and fornicators and murderers and idolaters, and every one who loves and practices falsehood."

How could I just enter there? — I with my smudged soul, sinful spirit, unclean thoughts, with the soiled robe of my life. How could I just enter *there?*

I do not share the belief some Christians have in a place called purgatory. But I can well imagine how such an idea could arise. One reason is psychological. We stand at the grave of a loved one or a friend with feelings of remorse: if only I had meant more to him or her.

If only I had done or said this or that. If only I could still do something to make up in some way for what I've done. But the dead person seems to be saying, It's too late. Impossible. And the gospels would also seem to say, Impossible; it's too late. The decision has been made.

There is also a religious reason for the idea of purgatory. How can a smudged sinner be here one moment and in glory — where neither sin nor uncleanness may enter — the next? The soul, it would seem, must first be cleansed, purged, and that cleansing takes place in purgatory. There, one does penance with temporary punishments. Just as the body must go through death and the grave in order to enter the new world, so the soul, it is argued, must be purified, "rebuilt." The soul must, so to speak, go through the "grave of souls."

On the basis of Christ's meritorious sacrifice and its lasting power, we say that at the time of rebirth the soul is essentially cleansed and that in the hour of death all evil that still remained within, falls away (Romans 7); that death is a dying of sin. At death, we become complete saints through Christ. And so I will be taken up in glory at the moment of death. This is possible (in contrast to the body, for which such is impossible) because the soul touches the invisible aspect of our being. Christ has been glorified invisibly, and now this *invisible* change can take place, already now, also in you and in me. We *are* and *shall be* glorified with him!

We have already given a lengthy answer to the Why with which we began. But one more thing remains to be said.

If we would be revealed visibly as children of God, already now, without seeing death, or by means of an immediate ascension, would not the very heart of the church be subjected to severe strain? Wouldn't the whole world then rush in to become members of the church? Wouldn't the number of self-centered and hypocritical Christians increase wildly? Wouldn't the faith-character of the congregation be threatened seriously (faith being the conviction of things *not seen,* Hebrews 11:1 tells us)? And wouldn't even more persons than do now, go to eternal death while imagining they are on the way to heaven?

Who wouldn't like to evade death? If Christendom presented visible assurance that you could escape death by joining the church, who wouldn't want to sign up? But to an unbelieving generation that asks for a sign, the Lord says, no other sign shall be given than that of Jonah the prophet (Matthew 12:38-42).

One way in which the sign of Jonah is given is the interment of Christian brothers and sisters. They die and are buried like Christ, like the unbelievers. I *believe* in the resurrection of the dead! I believe:

> When my body sinks in the earth
> — This is my faith's strong assurance —
> God prepares a place for me,
> turns believing into seeing.
> I'll escape the dust of earth,
> and see Christ eternally!

And so we die and are let down into the grave to disintegrate. How humiliating. But in this experience we may taste something, the "leftovers," of that complete suffering that was Christ Jesus' share. And so we also may become one with his death, in order that we may be glorified with him.

He "died." We "fall asleep." There's a world of difference between these two.

We do undergo a mild after-effect of *everything*

134

that was laid on him. We are to follow that path, so that our path will end more and more at his path and converge with it. For he is *the* Way. If we are willing to suffer with him, we shall also be glorified with him.

One who goes out through the gate with him will also be led back into the gate by him.

> Christ leads me through no darker rooms
> Than he went through before;
> And he that to God's kingdom comes
> Must enter by this door.
> — *Richard Baxter, 1681*

Now I think I know what Paul meant when he said death is "gain."

24. *At the Deathbed*

The Bible does not pay much attention to deathbeds. It seems to find it more important to inform us about the *life* of God's children rather than their death. We are told much about the life of Abraham, but nothing of his dying day. The Bible informs us extensively about Paul's missionary journeys, but about the circumstances under which he departed this life we are told exactly nothing. The same goes for Samuel, Peter, Isaiah, John. The Bible leads us into very few rooms that have death-beds. Among the few exceptions are those of Jacob, David and Elisha.

All of this is not to say that we must therefore turn our backs to all deathbeds and no longer talk about the subject. We may learn something from deathbeds. Frequently they tell us how dying persons have faced this moment. The folk expression "Everyone dies the kind of death that suits him best" contains a kernel of truth. In a person's last words and conversations his deepest emotions often are bared.

Let us in this conversation enter reverently some of the rooms in history in which deathbeds have been found.

We shall pass by the few familiar scenes of death mentioned in the Bible, except for one: the most remarkable, the most decisive one of all — the death of Jesus Christ. That death chamber was the universe. His deathbed was a cross. His friends "stood from afar"; his enemies stood close by and crowded around.

Most people are permitted to die in silence, with their beloved one at the bed. But Jesus also had to sign his own death certificate publicly; this deathbed concerned the entire world. So it was that at that moment he also made known, in his dying words, the deepest motive of his soul and revealed the immeasurable sense of this dying.

The seven last words on the cross always make me think of the candelabra in the temple. Whenever it became dark in God's house, those seven candles lit up and burned throughout the night. In that dark death chamber of Christ — dark, because of the riddle of this death, because of our sins and God's wrath — the seven candles in this golden candelabra, Jesus Christ, light up.

I'm not going to explain these seven last words. You are familiar with them from many sermons and meditations. But as you draw nearer, enter this death chamber often. Look and look again at that sevenfold light. You walk in the light when you follow that guide. Be mindful of this: only his dying glorifies me and remains the resting point of my heart.

Several centuries later, a woman named Monica lies on her deathbed. Her son, St. Augustine, spoke of her often in his *Confessions*. Utterly fatigued by high fever, she has become unconscious. When she comes back to consciousness, she asks, "Where am I?" She sees her loved ones deeply grieved around her bed. To them she says, "Bury your mother here." Someone answers, "Mother, but isn't it more comforting to you that you should die not in a strange land, but in your fatherland?"

Only a few days before, she had replied to a similar remark, "Nothing is far from God, and I need not fear that at the end of the ages he would not know the place where he will resurrect me." Now she says, "Bury this body where you will; I only ask this of you, that you remember me before the altar of the Lord, wherever you may be."

From this last remark we see the need to put the last words even of devout believers to the test of the Word of God, for they are not always infallible. The thought we find expressed in Monica's words, to intercede for the dead before the altar, is not biblical. I once met a believing woman who never took part in the celebration of Holy Communion. "My mother," she explained to me, "said on her death bed, 'Child, remember never to go to the Lord's Table.'" Believing people can, in their dying moments, say the wrong thing.

Monica dies on the ninth day of her illness. Augustine wrote afterwards, "Thus . . . in the fifty-sixth year of her life, in the thirty-third year of my life, her godly and pious soul was delivered from the body."

No one but the doctor and the nurse was allowed to enter the death chamber of St. Augustine. He had parted with the clergy earlier. But on his deathbed, he did not dare to make his own those words he had spoken in farewell to his teacher Ambrose, and that he had quoted so often: "I haven't lived in such a manner that I should be ashamed to live among you yet longer. But neither do I fear to die, for we have a good Father." On the contrary, St. Augustine retreated to the death chamber.

There, he remained alone for ten days, his eyes fixed on quires of parchment and on psalms of penitence that he had nailed to the walls, repeating the words over and over, and continually weeping. And so he died.

He did not have a last will and testament. This poor one for God's sake had no earthly goods to divide. He only left a large library, the "archives of a genius."

Now we enter the room in which John Calvin died. He has been lying there dying almost a year. But lying, really, is not the correct word. Though tormented by many diseases and severe ailments which pulled him toward the grave, Calvin kept working to the very last moment. He walked, stood dying, one almost could say. His desire was that God would find him watchful and at work. But in the end he could not leave the house any more. He attended a fraternal banquet with his colleagues on May 17. At that meal he tried to be cheerful, but he had to be carried away from the table. He called the magistrate to his bed to confess his guilt: "My violent feelings displease me greatly."

On April 25 he had dictated his will. Some flashes from that document: "In the name of God, I, John Calvin, minister of the divine Word at the church of Geneva, weakened by many and varied illnesses... thank God that he not only has shown mercy upon me, his poor creature, and...has been tolerant with me in all my sins and weaknesses, but, what is far more, that he has granted me the grace to serve him through my labors.... I declare, that I wish to live and die in this faith that he has given me, whereas I have no other hope or refuge than his election in which my salvation is rooted. I embrace the grace that he has prepared for me in Jesus, our Lord, and accept the merit of his suffering and death, through which all my sins be buried...."

Regarding the property he leaves behind, some dispositions are included in the will. A cousin David, who has been "puffed up" and "frivolous," gets only 25 crowns; his sisters receive 30 crowns. But the property he is able to will to his survivors amounts to almost nothing. Calvin stipulated for his funeral that his body should be wrapped in a white sheet and placed in a simple pine coffin. He wanted no speeches or songs at the graveside, no stone on his grave.

On May 2 the struggle with death began. Emaciated to the bone, Calvin suffered innumerable pains. Repeatedly he was heard sighing the words from Psalm 39, "I am dumb, I do not open my mouth; for it is thou who hast done it." During that time he still gave the farewell banquet for his colleagues. On May 27, 1556, he died. When his friend Beza came to see him, because Calvin's spirit had seemed to revive for a moment, he had already died. "Just like the sun goes down," Beza later remarked. "After he has given us an example of an irreproachable life, he now also gives us an example of a courageous and Christian death."

That night the city of Geneva was filled with laments.

The third room we shall enter is Luther's. The room was far from the place where he lived, as he was busy settling a quarrel between rulers at his place of birth. Though his death did not come unexpectedly, certainly not to his wife, who had premonitions (her expressions of concern were negated by her husband with a note of humor), it came rather suddenly.

He had an attack of angina. He could not finish the preaching of the word on Sunday. On his deathbed, in the presence of rulers and friends, he spoke several texts:

"Father, into thy hands I commit my spirit," Luther said, when he lay down for the last time. And also: "I thank you, God, Father of our Lord Jesus Christ, that you have revealed unto me your dear son in whom I believe, whom I have loved, preached, confessed and glorified...." To the question whether he would die in that faith, he answered, clearly, "Yes." Then, turning on his right side, he exhaled his last breath. It was 3 o'clock, February 18, 1546. At his funeral, the congregation wept more than it sang.

We also enter briefly the room where John Bunyan died. Silence has fallen in the quiet room where the author of *Pilgrim's Progress* is soon to die.

He speaks softly about prayer, about the value of Sunday ("the market-day for the soul"), about suffering. Someone asks a question about suffering. He says, "I often have thought that the best Christians are born in the worst times and that undoubtedly we are not better Christians because we are not oppressed. Who was ever as saintly as Noah and Lot in days of temptation, and who was as reckless and frivolous as they were in days of prosperity?" Dying, he speaks of the joys of heaven that he already seems with his mind's eye to see. "Saints in the world to come" were the last words of his anyone heard.

Long before Dwight L. Moody died, he had said, "When the press boys call, 'Moody is dead,' don't believe it. At that time I shall live more than ever." On his deathbed, on December 22, 1899, he said, "The earth disappears. The heavens open up." And, "I have tried to leave behind as much as possible; not money or wealth, but much work. This is my glorification. This is my day of coronation. For many years I have looked forward to this day."

J. H. Gunning (I do not include his title or identify

him further, for what good is that in the hour of death?) wrote a letter with "last words" in the event he would be unable to speak just before dying. He was in bed, surrounded by books, but only one book still talked to him: the Bible. He laid his hands in a blessing on those who visited him. He expected to hear from them a word of life from the Book of Life. When he was commended to God before his death, as he had requested, he said, "This is what comforts me and only this." The last word from his mouth was a threefold "Amen" to the text "Whoever believes in the Son has eternal life — he shall never see death."

Finally, that great statesman, Abraham Kuyper.

Idenburg, his friend, stands at the bedside. This is their conversation:

"The Lord is with you, isn't he?"

"Yes," Kuyper whispers with great certainty.

"Shall I tell our people that God is your refuge and strength?"

Again that certain whisper, "Yes, in ... all ... respects. ..."

"Just this morning we read from Psalm 46, 'God is our refuge and strength, a very present help in trouble.' "

Kuyper nodded in a happy smile, and a moment later said, "I ... thank ... you ... for ... everything."

And so also this great statesman and theologian went, as a poor sinner, trusting in God's mercy.

One could write an entire book about the deathbeds of silence — and another about the deathbeds of unbelievers. That is not our intention here. The question is merely: where and how will you die?

What will your deathbed be like? Or will there be none? Will you be found dead in your chair? Will you be found collapsed on the street? Who can tell? No one knows. But that isn't the most important thing.

The important thing is whether your wedding garment is ready. Time was when many trousseaux contained a death shirt. I hardly think I would bother with that. But the wedding garment should be ready. We may not arrive in a borrowed suit. The wedding garment has to be our aim — the garment the Bridegroom gives us, one that he weaves for us by using our fingers, by using our faith that yields good works. That garment is one of humility and justice.

25. Last Respects

As a boy I had no interest in knowing where or how I would be buried some day. This has changed as I have grown older.

I can understand that older people, who contemplate soberly the things that inevitably face them, may have questions about burial. I've often had to answer questions in this area, and so we shall devote this conversation to that subject.

I know some — not many, to be sure — older Christians who incline toward cremation. Let us be careful not to label them for this reason as godless. We have received no special command from God to bury all people. But I do think that the custom of burial has some good things to be said for it and should be preserved as long as possible.

What about funeral services?

As far as dress is concerned, there are two extremes: all is black, or all is white. At the funeral of one who has fallen asleep in Jesus, I consider neither extreme quite appropriate. At such a funeral not everything is black, is it? One day a taxicab took me to the house of a deceased person.

"Life is full of sharp contrasts, Sir," the talkative driver began. "I just had some newlyweds in this car. To tell you the truth, I just stuck the flowers under the seat."

I replied that in this case the contrast was not quite as sharp as he might think; that I was going to the home of someone who had longed for many weeks to be with Jesus. And now she was at the wedding feast.

Indeed, at such a funeral not everything is black and dark. But not everything is white and light, either. We are temporarily separated from loved ones who pass away. That separation causes grief and darkness.

At a Christian funeral, both darkness and light must come to expression. Usually darkness is present. But light should also fall on that funeral — in the form of a palm branch, a sober floral piece (not a "sea of flowers"), a song of hope and faith. The light and the dark can be balanced at the funeral service particularly by what the minister says.

I should like to have written in my obituary: "No speeches." If words must be spoken at all, let them be spoken by one of your best friends or by members of the family who have really known you or by the minister. The message of such words should center around the grace of God.

The service should be conducted by the clergyman, perhaps first at the home of the deceased with a *brief,* personal, and heartfelt word. At the service in church he should proclaim the Lord of death and life as he also revealed himself in the deceased one. At the graveside the minister should recite words like those of the song:

When my body sinks in the earth
— This is my faith's strong assurance —
God prepares a place for me,
Turns my faith into beholding.
I'll escape the dust of earth,
And see Christ eternally!

He should also recite the creed, request the singing of a song (a favorite of the one who has died), and conclude with the Lord's Prayer.

Everything that would tend to lengthen the service and play on the emotions to an even greater extent than the mere fact of death should be avoided. Let the pallbearers, for example, go toward the grave immediately after they lift the casket.

Do you want a stone on your grave? Do not decide on that yourself. Allow the love of your friends who remain to carve out that stone. I read once about a sale of gravestones. A collector who went to the sale remembered that he had never seen such a fine collection. When he asked why the sale was being held, the answer came that all these stones had been ordered and custom-made, but were never picked up. By the time they were ready, the ones for whose graves they had been meant were forgotten.

But let it not be a stone that is to keep alive your memory. I am thinking of a poem Guido Gezelle, the Flemish poet, wrote about his mother:

Of you,
my mother dear
who lies here
no likeness
was painted
no sculpture hewn
no drawing

no etching
no chiseled stone
only that likeness
of you in me
is left behind.

Never may I
unworthily
spoil your image
but may it be
alive in me
and some day
die with me.

Today's world thinks differently about that which remains. If you walk in Paris on a Sunday morning, you cannot help noticing that the subways and buses pour out people over certain spots. For a moment you may think that there is a church service in the area. A service, yes, but not a church service. These people are going to a cemetery, armed with flowers. They no longer see the inside of a church on Sunday, but in the churchyard they feel at home like children. The Living One no longer occupies the central place in their lives, but the dead ones rate a visit each Sunday. Cemeteries turn into beautiful flower gardens. I once stood at the casket of a child who had died in an accident. For a moment I thought I was standing at a flowerbox. The child was no longer visible. All I could see was flowers. That is the way of graveyards.

Blessed are we when we may know that our deceased loved ones are with the Living One; when we can say of them in the churchyard what the angel said in the garden on the first Easter morning: "They are not here...."

When we know them to be with Jesus, that spot, that plot, does not mean everything to us. Nor do we continue to visit them there, nor do we address the dead in the coffin at the funeral (as I have all too often heard). I find quite distasteful a story I heard at a recent funeral at which, after the last farewell speech, it was announced that finally the deceased one would have something to say. A tape recorder was turned on, and his recorded voice sounded over his own grave.

Remain sober and truthful. Look forward to seeing your loved ones above or in the new earth. They have gone ahead of us.

> We are traveling home to God,
> In the way the fathers trod:
> They are happy now, and we
> Soon their happiness shall see.
> — *John Cerrick, 1742*

BEHIND THE DOOR

26. Totally Different

During the Middle Ages a story was told about two pilgrims who met daily to speak about life in heaven. One had even more beautiful visions of heaven than the other. But neither could guarantee that his image of the life hereafter was entirely correct. The two agreed that the first of them to die would return briefly to tell the other how accurate their pictures of eternal life had been.

And so, shortly after the one died, he appeared to the other, who asked, *"Taliter qualiter?"*, that is, is it as we have spoken of it? The answer was, *"Totaliter aliter"*: totally different.

Keeping this answer in mind, we should talk for a moment about life behind that door to eternity, about being in those halls of happiness. Fantasies about heaven may be pious and sweet, but when we look back, it will become evident that everything is totally different from what people have imagined. Much talk about heaven is merely the philosophizing of a caterpillar about the glory of being a butterfly.

We should stick closely to what the Bible says about

151

these matters. We may be certain that the half of it is not told us here, that we will understand it hereafter. When Paul was lifted up to the third heaven (2 Corinthians 12), he saw indescribable things; he could never put into words anything about them. So majestic and impressive was his vision that he actually could not absorb what he saw, much less express what he saw in human language.

And there is Lazarus, whom Jesus raised from the dead. We may assume, I think, that his spirit was with God before he arose: he was truly dead. But Lazarus does not speak one word of what he has seen and heard. Though Lazarus usually does not open his mouth to speak — he is the quiet type who sits silently in your presence — couldn't he just once have talked after his return to life?

I suspect that Lazarus did not remember much of his being dead. His earthly thinking could not comprehend and retain that glory. Under certain conditions we can, here on earth, experience such traumatic things that afterwards we cannot seem to remember them. I think this may also be the reason that so little has been told us about heaven. We cannot comprehend it, we cannot yet absorb it.

God likes surprises. He still has great and beautiful things in store for us. We should not try to open that surprise package before it is time. Let us be satisfied with the announcement. Soon the horn of plenty will be poured out before our feet.

And so we shall not speak extensively in this book about the little that is known of heaven. Other books have dealt with that subject. We shall present only some brief flashes in the few concluding conversations.

First, I would like to say that you should view heaven as an intermediate state, a stopover rather than a destination. Heaven is an interlude, not the end. We ought not to think that in heaven the last milestone has been reached and no more changes will take place after that.

Notice what happens at Jesus' ascension as the disciples gaze toward the heavens. So attentively do they concentrate that at first they do not notice the two angels who have descended inaudibly like snowflakes falling on dark clumps of earth. Suddenly they hear from the mouth of the angels, "Men of Galilee, why do you stand looking into heaven? This Jesus, who was taken up from you into heaven, will come in the same way as you saw him go into heaven" (Acts 1:11). The angels draw the disciples' attention away from heaven back to earth. Here the finale will take place; here joy will be *forever*.

Heaven will come down to earth, because Jesus and God-in-Christ shall come to earth to pitch their tents among God's people, to be all in all — forever. The Bible states that the meek shall inherit *the earth* — not heaven but the earth!

Heaven is not the very last; it is the next-to-last.

Everything moves toward the glorification of this world. One day, Christ will come down with all the saints and the holy angels; and a great heavenly invasion will take place on the earth. Then the earth will be covered with the knowledge of his name, as the waters that cover the seas.

But may we not then long for heaven? Of course. During World War II, the Queen of the Netherlands fled to England. But while she was there every underground worker felt honored to be called to England. Every red-blooded Hollander was eager to see his queen there. How much more meaningful, though, it was to her subjects when they could greet their queen again on native soil. So, too, it is an honor, a "gain," to be lifted up in glory at the present time. Do we not live far removed from the Lord on the present earth? Then we shall "live in" with him. Now we are guests in a strange land; soon, we shall be home. But that home is not the last dwelling place. That final dwelling place will again be on the earth, the new earth.

Do not loosen your ties to the earth because of heaven.

But also do not loosen your ties to heaven because of the earth.

Behind the door to eternity, eternal bliss, glory, flows in your direction. That glory is so overwhelming that one can only speak of it in figurative language. Nobody can say exactly what it is.

How will it be
when that light shining from the Father's house
meets us at last,
and we, tired of wandering,
having finished the difficult fight,
enter the door to eternity?

How will it be
when we shake the dust off our feet
and the last pearls of sweat
are wiped off our brows;
when we see that wholeness
and greet that redemption
that so often renewed our pilgrim hope?

How will it be
when we walk in the light
that lifts all mists eternally;
when we for the first time see

ourselves, free, cleansed of sin
through eyes no longer breaking in death?

How will it be
when we, glorified, walk into God's mansion, our home;
when no curse casts us out,
no sin torments us,
and we walk in that city
where redeemed sinners live?

How will it be
when we hear his voice calling,
"Come, you blessed of the Father,"
when we see him face to face,
shout for joy before his throne?

How will it be
when we see those eyes
that once wept for his people
and for their souls' agony;
when we see those wounds
that once spilled precious blood
which bought us and freed us
from eternal death?

Yes — how will it be, for us?

St. John, the old visionary, was allowed to have a brief view through the door to eternity. In the last book of the Bible he presents what he saw, but he does not do so in a logical discourse. He paints a picture for us. He *shows* us through his eyes. What does he see?

He sees many things, but one thing stands out: the throne of God. That throne is the center around which everything is concentrated. That throne draws all of John's attention. The splendor that goes forth from it is so overwhelming, and the glitter of something like a glass sea around the throne so blinding, that John actually cannot see God. He sees only the shining reflection, which reminds him of diamonds. Even John's sanctified, inspired eye could not see God in a vision. So great is God's glory that no eye has ever seen it.

That is the heart of what heaven will be like: *we shall see God.* Before that reality we can only be still in amazement: to see God and not to be lost; to see God and *live.*

We shall never be weary of looking at him; for we shall never see everything. We shall fall from one ecstasy into the next. We forget time and place. We *live,* in the deepest, most intense sense of the word.

One to whom God is not everything, to whom he is not the center of his desires, will not feel at home in heaven, nor will he enter there.

John also sees Jesus crowned with honor and glory, the Lion of Judah and yet also the Lamb, the lion-lamb. "And between the throne and the four living creatures and among the elders, I saw a Lamb standing, as though it had been slain . . ." (Revelation 5:6).

At the present time I must still believe, speak, and write in him and about him whom I have never *seen.* I feel what might almost be called a sacred jealousy toward those who did see him: Peter, John, Paul. Yes, I know: his ascension was beneficial for us, but it also presents a point of loss: now we do not see him. In this life here on earth, he has never again been seen. But one who enters the door to eternity will see him as he is.

To enter heaven and to see Jesus; to enjoy the company of the Redeemer. When I think of that, a strong desire to be there gets hold of me.

But now we still have some questions. How will it be, how shall *we* be, once we are there? As long as the day of judgment is not here, we do not have our renewed bodies. Will we recognize each other there? Will we be able to be happy if one of us, a child, a spouse, a dear friend, is missed up there?

A quiet professor once walked with his host along the beach. The host, attempting to draw him out, asked, "Professor, how shall it be when one day that passage, 'And the sea was no more,' will be fulfilled?"

"Wait and see," the professor replied.

That reply could also serve for the above questions, especially the first one — how will it be.

When Scripture speaks of eternal life, it says very little about the condition of individual believers. The Bible views these things in the larger context of the Kingdom of God. The attention of the Bible is focused so much on that impressive end — the judgment and the return of Christ — that very little is mentioned of concrete details regarding the heavenly interlude. People, even believers, do not form the center.

If we keep that in mind, we may spend a little time thinking about the other questions we mentioned.

If I have difficulty thinking of a resurrection body as being a spiritual body (1 Corinthians 15) — without differences in sex, without a stomach — how can I imagine that existence without a body? No one is able to tell you that. Yet John sees the saints in long white robes. Yet Jesus says that Lazarus is in the bosom of Abraham. Let that be sufficient for us.

I already have arrived at the second question, that of *recognition*. Usually one hears "No" to that question. I have never quite felt at ease with that answer. Don't God's children make up a community? Has not he established a *covenant* with his people, and aren't members of Christ therefore also members of each other? If this is true here and now, wouldn't it be true in a much richer measure in heaven above?

On the basis of that covenant communion with the

Lord, I venture to say that we shall certainly not move past each other as shadowy ghosts without any bond or recognition.

Doesn't the Old Testament speak time and again of those who are dying as being "gathered unto their fathers" (for example, 1 Kings 11:43). Doesn't Lazarus recline in the bosom of Abraham? Doesn't David say that he will go to the baby that has died, but that the child, born of his affair with Bathsheba, will not come back to him (2 Samuel 12:23)? And when the congregation at Thessalonica sat in ashes, covered with sackcloth, each time death took one of their members from among them, so that they could not meet the Lord *together*, Paul said, "We shall not precede those who have fallen asleep." They shall rise first, and then we who are alive shall be caught up with them to meet the Lord.

It is not correct, therefore, to say that the Bible is completely silent on this subject. It is not. It must yet be said that our *recognizing* will be more in the sense of *acknowledging* than in the sense of showing acquaintance with someone. We will look completely different, and our seeing and knowing will be different, for they will no longer be seeing and knowing in part.

How well do we really know each other here? Come to think of it, our knowledge of our spouse, our children, our friends — even of ourselves — is quite faltering. How different all this will be then. No doubt we shall see some people to whom we had accorded a prominent place in the last rows, and vice versa. There we shall know as we are known here by God. For that reason, too, heaven will be full of surprises. It will not merely be a continuation of this earthly busyness. We shall be completely changed, remade after God's likeness. We shall recognize, *acknowledge,* each other!

And so, when I enter into God's glory, I shall see

him. But I hope also to make my acquaintance with Abraham, the father of us all in the faith, with Peter and John, with Calvin and Luther, with Moody and Sankey, and with my own father and mother who have fallen asleep in Jesus, together, with all of these, to shout forth the name of the Lord!

But one other question arises: when we meet and recognize each other up yonder, how can heaven still be heaven if we discover that one of our loved ones is not there and therefore must be in hell. Will our joy not be overshadowed with sadness?

This question has no easy answer. We can say that our lives ought to be so full of the recognition of God that we can acknowledge he is just — even if one of our loved ones should go to eternal punishment. Perhaps when one day we see him in all his majesty and splendor and become aware of how our loved one has resisted him, stepped on his name, or passed him by with a shrug of the shoulders, we shall be able to say: The Lord is just in his way and in his work — Hallelujah! Perhaps at that time we shall be able to hate those who hate God; they will be like enemies to us. God will have to be all and in all, also in us. Only then it will be possible for us to accept this — and not without his being everything.

We must still touch one important point. The great abyss between heaven and hell becomes visible through the opened door. Crossing over is impossible.

C. S. Lewis's book *The Great Divorce* is based on an old legend in which those who are condemned in hell are allowed to enter heaven once, for a brief moment. Lewis has the condemned travel to heaven in a modern tour bus. In this strange story one genuine biblical teach-

ing is given striking expression: every one of the condemned wants to go back to hell. They have the same sins
and shortcomings that evoked their verdict in the first
place. For that reason none of them feels at home in
heaven. The dwellers in hell remain in their sins. They
blaspheme God, as John sees in one of his visions. They
are stooped and hardened by evil. No one calls for
grace. If anyone should call for grace, God would bridge
the deepest abyss, but nobody calls. The rich man of
Jesus' parable did not cry out because of repentance
and conversion, but out of pain and irritation and self-
centeredness. Many of the complaints about a God who
eternally punishes fall away when seen against that background. One must look at this problem of guilt from the
viewpoint of the condemned who *remains* rebellious, who
never asks for grace and therefore remains under the
judgment. The abyss is present. No one should pretend
it isn't, as people often do today. The Bible shows the
abyss clearly.

Moreover, John was allowed a view of heaven
through the door of eternity, but not of hell. Let us look
through his eyes, in a manner of speaking. Let us direct
our eyes and hearts toward heaven.

How beautiful it must be there. Indeed:

> What no eye has seen
> nor ear heard,
> nor in the heart of a man
> was conceived,
> God has prepared for those
> who love him (1 Cor. 2:9).

> And behold,
> the half was not told me! (1 Kings 10:7).

27. Judgment

The Bible reflects much more extensively on the events of the day of the last judgment than on the heavenly interlude. For that reason we shall devote two conversations to that last day.

Through the open door John also saw the judgment seat and the last judgment. He pictures the scene with these words:

> Then I saw a great white throne and him who sat upon it; from his presence earth and sky fled away, and no place was found for them. And I saw the dead, great and small, standing before the throne, and books were opened. Also another book was opened, which is the book of life. And the dead were judged by what was written in the books, by what they had done. And the sea gave up the dead in it, Death and Hades gave up the dead in them, and all were judged by what they had done. Then Death and Hades were thrown into the lake of fire. This is the second death, the lake of fire; and if any one's name was not found written in the book of life, he was thrown into the lake of fire (Revelation 20:11-15).

This vision is one of the last John saw. Like a film which suddenly zooms in on one person whose image fills the entire screen and so provokes awe and draws all our attention, so the screen of John's vision projects images for our view. When the last trumpet is lifted to the mouth of the player, the earth and heaven fall away and the throne, large and forceful, and he who sits on it flash onto John's screen.

Everything moves toward that scene.

The throne is large, because the judgment will be great, encompassing the entire world, and inescapable.

The throne is white, because the sentence will be without error or spot.

Jesus sits on the throne. No longer does he stand in humiliation before an earthly judge; now he himself is the judge who appears in majesty. Earth and heaven cannot stand his presence; they disappear, only to re-appear later in new forms. No one escapes this judgment. John sees the dead. Mortals (and who among us will not sleep the sleep of death?) great and small stand before the throne.

Great and small: the esteemed and the despicable, the well-known and the unknown, kings and presidents, known all over the world, and the humblest citizen on the back street, known only to the neighbors. No one is exempted. All come to stand before that throne. No matter where we have died, we shall be drawn toward the judgment seat at that time when the earth and the sea disappear from his presence. "I *saw*," John says. I can almost see his startled face when he sees those millions and millions of people. . . . You, too, will take your place there!

The trial follows.

Witnesses for and against are not being called to the

stand. Their presence is not necessary. God has kept record of everything, including the last word and the last act. The books are opened which bring everything to light. One could say in today's language, "God's tape recorders have picked up everything in its smallest detail."

"The books were opened." God's books and our hearts converge.

> My heart is like an open daybook in God's hand;
> He pages through my book and reads and reads,
> searches and finds in every far corner
> whatever between these covers has appeared.

The same figure of speech is used here as that in the text, "We must be revealed before the judgment seat." The books are opened: the masks fall, the veils are removed, our designs are brought to light. Those who have shouted from pulpits, "To God alone be glory!" may be exposed as little, ambitious men whose aim has been their own glory. Those well-known as generous philanthropists may be exposed as selfish persons who were really interested only in their own good. Other people will look surprised when they are told, "Child, go in, enter into the joy of your Lord." "Who, *me?*" they will say. . . .

One day some women were visiting together. The hostess had hidden a tape recorder under one of the chairs, which she disclosed later in the visit, and played back the tape in their presence. How embarrassed they were when they heard themselves talking about so many small, insignificant things.

One day God will play back the tape of your life. Then what? Do not think that thousands of people will receive a mass sentence all at once. The proceedings will take place on a personal basis. "Everyone shall be judged according to his works."

Can this be carried out? Is it practically possible? Will the processing and judging of millions upon millions of people not take ages, even centuries? The answer to that is another question: is anything impossible with God?

I've been told by people who barely escaped death that they saw their entire lives pass before their eyes in one split second. On the last day, on the borders of time and eternity, one may perhaps see his life pass in such a flash.

No matter how this will happen, the Bible makes it clear that we shall be judged personally, without exception.

What is the verdict? What is the sentence?

But before that, first a question I am frequently asked: "Must we be judged twice? Isn't there already a judgment at death?"

Yes, one could even speak of a triple judgment. One who hears the word of God and does not believe, already has been judged, Jesus states. But that judgment is not final. As long as a person is alive, he can repent from unbelief. Should you still be in need of that repentance, I plead with you to hurry for your life's sake.

At the moment of death the judgment becomes final. At that moment I lift up my eyes either as the rich man in eternal pain or as Lazarus safe in the arms of Jesus forever. But this judgment, this decision, is private, not public. On the last judgment day that verdict will be repeated and spoken publicly. It is that decision which John sees and hears. What is it?

First, death and death's domain are cast into the lake of fire, into the outer-cosmic region: the place for what has been banished eternally from God's presence and counts never again. Death, decay, sorrow, pain, misery, war, quarrels, tears, grief are cast away for all eternity, never to return.

But then, to that region all those whose names are not written in the other book, in the "book of life," will also be referred. Notice: it is our own book which accuses us. Those thousands of books, that large library, are full of deadly letters.

But — thanks be to God — among these many books of death John sees another strange book: the daybook of Jesus. And at this time it also becomes evident that the final Judge is also the only Preserver. Only the one whose name is written in the book of life shall enter into the joy of the Lord.

And thus all stand before that white throne. No one walks or runs away. No one objects. The process is pure and perfect.

In the background I imagine angels playing mighty organs that give melody to the words, "Yea, Lord God the Almighty, true and just are thy judgments!"

I fall to the ground.

I shall plead for my Judge's mercy, because there suddenly I see that his mighty hands are pierced. I begin to see that the radiant Judge is exactly the same as he who first gave himself over to the cross for my sake.

God, have mercy.

Brother, sister, do you *know* whether your name is written in his book? Your eternal well-being or woe depends on it.

Once during Christ's ministry on earth his followers were excited that they had even been able to cast out demons. Calm down, Jesus said. "Rejoice much more about this, that your names are written in the book of life of the Lamb" (Luke 10:20).

That's the most important of all.

That's the most beautiful of all!

How do I know my name is written in the book?

The Canons of Dort, whose doctrinal teaching is based on Scripture, speak of degrees of assurance, and of various measures by which I bring forth the fruit of faith.

I may live in a firmly grounded hope as I discover with joy that I cling to God's promises, that I am aware of my guilt and long for God, that I feel the need for prayer and that I am eager to serve him. Or, to say the same in biblical words, "One who believes in the Son has eternal life."

With the Psalmist I may express that confidence and that hope:

> I believe that I shall see
>   the goodness of the Lord
>   in the land of the living!
> Wait for the Lord; be strong,
>   and let your heart take courage;
>   Yea, wait for the Lord! (Psalm 27:13-14).

28. A Happy Prospect

I don't know if you read contemporary novels. If so, you'll probably agree that a mood of pessimism is quite prominent in literature today. One reads in these books how life in this world ends in a dark nothingness, in a miserable empty space. In a novel of some years ago entitled *The Pilgrimage,* a boat full of migrants struck a mine. All but one of the passengers drowned. God, helpless, wept, and his tears came down in mighty torrents on the ocean, making it even more difficult for the drowning ones to save their lives. The one survivor of the incident was a very ugly girl who was leaving the country because she felt people were always staring at her because she was so ugly. The author seems to say that whatever is left of this life is ugliness and misery.

Many more such examples could be cited. We shall not do so here. Instead, we can summarize this in the poet's complaint:

> We seek you behind the horizon,
> age upon age, hour upon hour.

167

We are but some vague, black shadows
that die out slowly
against your fountain of fire.

Nevertheless, Christian faith which has a look inside the open door sees even in the most difficult times a panorama of that beautiful end.

That faith knows that the last word is not going under, not an earth scorched black by war, not the chaos of nothingness. The end toward which everything is moving is a happy wedding, an eternal feast.

The last thing John sees on the screen of his visions is the new Jerusalem.

> And I saw a new heaven and a new earth; for the first heaven and the first earth had passed away, and the sea was no more. And I saw the holy city, new Jerusalem, coming down out of heaven from God, prepared as a bride adorned for her husband ... (Revelation 21:1-3).

Let us take a look at this panorama, in the joyful expectation that someday we may see it in reality and enter it.

John sees the new life toward which everything moves portrayed in two scenes: the picture of a city and the picture of a garden, Jerusalem and Paradise.

City and garden: what a contrast. The one is the monument of culture, of creative human hands that have molded and formed God's gifts but often disfigured and deformed them as well. The garden, Paradise, is as a part of nature a monument to the direct creative acts of God.

Man's work and God's work contrast starkly in this life. Man today is pulled from one to the other. The exodus from the farm to the city has added to the immense problems of the city. Conversely, city-dwellers move, particularly during vacations, from the city to the outdoors.

This contrast no longer exists in eternity. The city is populated like a village, and the world has become one city, in which the highest culture is being enjoyed. That culture is in no way contrary to God's creative works. God and man meet together peacefully in a holy harmony.

And so John sees — and we see over his shoulders — that this is a *holy* city. A holy *city*. To our thinking this may seem like a strange contradiction. Do not sin and injustices mount in the city?

I remember once reading the story of a sailor who spent most of his life on the fresh seas and breathed pure air for many years. When he returned to his birthplace, a large city, he first bumped into a drunk. Then at a street corner a prostitute accosted him. Finally, he found a boarding house to stay in. But the couple who owned the house argued and fought continuously. The woman was a neurotic, screaming loudly at night. The man killed her one night, choking her between the pillows. The sailor could not stand Babylon any longer and returned to the pure waters.

The city — *the* place of misery, sin and dirt. . . .

But the new Jerusalem will be holy and without sin. It comes from heaven. From that city God comes to sanctify the world. One will find neither sinner nor sin in that new city. "But as for the cowardly, the faithless, the polluted, as for murderers, fornicators, sorcerers, idolaters, and all liars, their lot shall be in the lake that burns with fire and brimstone . . . ," in a place far removed from the new, holy city.

And thus, this panorama also presents to you and me

a serious warning. We are to wash our garments in the blood of him who cleanses from sin.

Because this world-city is holy, John sees that it is beautiful and clean. Today, beauty and art may seem to be the possession of the unholy. But essentially only those things are beautiful and pure which are also holy. The Old Testament sage has said that a deceitful woman without discretion is like a gold ring in a swine's snout (Proverbs 11:22). Godliness and beauty belong together.

The new world will sparkle like a crystal-clear diamond. A diamond catches the light, holds it, and reflects it. Similarly, the new Jerusalem, God's new mankind and his new world, absorbs that divine light and transmits it. Everything there is filled with his glory.

Take a look: the streets are of gold, the cement in the walls is made of diamond, and the foundations are made of precious stones. John is of course using only figurative language. The reality will be even more beautiful. What is most valuable here (the standard of our currency), gold, is used there as pavement. That which costs thousands of dollars here, diamond, is used there, in a manner of speaking, as cement!

The psychology of colors has been studied carefully in recent years. Particular colors have been found to create particular moods in people. Some colors are believed to increase production, while others appear to reduce efficiency. In the new Jerusalem we shall see the most beautiful harmony of colors. Each of the twelve precious stones of Revelation 21 has a distinctly different color. Seeing God's color chart will cause us to praise him endlessly.

No, we shall not merely sing. We also shall *see* in endless ecstasy. Even now, a beautiful sunset can keep us spellbound and make us forget time. Much more the reality reflected in John's vision.

The new world is holy, beautiful, glorious, and also *safe*. The gates are open in all directions during the day and at night. On each gate the imposing figure of an angel, of a heavenly guard, guarantees safety. No unrest will disturb the city. War, battles, quarrels, discord, have forever been removed from the earth.

We are going to the Freedom Celebration, to the Feast of Peace, that will end nevermore.

> Jerusalem! high tower thy glorious walls,
> > Would to God I were in thee!
> Desire of thee my longing heart enthralls,
> > Desire at home to be;
> Wide from the world outleaping,
> > O'er hill and vale and plain,
> My soul's strong wing is sweeping
> > Thy portals to attain.
> > > *— J. M. Meyfart, 1626*

This city will also be the City of Light, because God is there. He is the Light, and darkness does not dwell in him. Street lighting often creates a problem for the modern city. I can recall, as a youth, the lamplighter walking through the streets with his stepladder. The lamps he lit have been obsolete for many years, with the rise of electric lights. But one day even the sun and moon will become obsolete, the Bible says: "And the city has no need of sun or moon to shine upon it, for the glory of God is its light, and its lamp is the Lamb. By its light shall the nations walk. . . ."

And all my fountains shall be in him. It shouldn't be surprising that in this city crystal-clear water of life shoots upward, and that here one finds parks and gardens, for this is Paradise. He is here.

We shall honor him in the new Paradise. His name shall be on our foreheads.

Nearer, ever nearer,
Christ, we draw to thee,
Deep in adoration
Bending low the knee.
Great and ever greater
Are thy mercies here;
True and everlasting
Are the glories here.
Clearer still, and clearer,
Dawns the light from heaven
In our sadness bringing
News of sins forgiven.
Onward, ever onward,
Journeying over the road,
Trod by saints before us,
Journeying on to God.
Bliss, all bliss excelling,
When the ransomed soul,
Earthly toils forgetting,
Finds its promised goal.
(after Godfrey Thring, 1862)

Modern man has no outlook. He would rather not look ahead. He is preoccupied with the here and now. Yet, we know that the world is coming to an end. The signs of the return of Jesus are growing clearer and ever more urgent. Apostasy increases. Wars have extended from regional to continental wars, and from continental wars they grow into world wars. By modern transportation and technology, the gospel is reaching the farthest corners of the earth. The spirit of Antichrist thrusts onward ever more. In short, "Children, the hour has come."

My brother and sister, in your life, too, the evening has fallen. As your hair is greying, the signs of your life's end become more pronounced. Look, look more often at that beautiful panorama toward which everything moves. Praise the Lord for that. May that prospect comfort you in the evening of your life. The Holy Spirit wants to comfort you particularly with that vision at a time when this earthly life passes you by increasingly.

The body that grows older stoops toward the earth. But let the spirit be lifted up. Allow the Holy Spirit to put you on a high mountain, as he did John. From that vantage point the outlook is good and beautiful.

From those mountains of prayer and faith, of hope and of love, the song comes into the evening of your life:

> As I draw nearer
> to the house of my Father,
> I yearn more and more
> for the heavenly mansion,
> where after life's battle
> my King's blessing awaits.
>
> What hinders me yet?
> I shall go to God's children.
> I hear now the glad sounds
> of heavenly servants,
> who jubilantly call me
> to my Father's house.

29. *A Final Note*

And so we have, in our thoughts, sat down together.

I hope that these conversations have sustained you and have been of help on your way to the door to eternity.

And though we have most likely never met in this life, may God grant that we meet before his throne.

I hope that this book contributes in such a way that when the last hour comes, you may say:

> As I stand on the verge of life,
> I view the scene on either hand.
> My spirit longs to be with God,
> my body to rest in this land.
> Earth, do not bind my heart to you,
> It is far better to depart,
> to lay me down to sleep in him
> who is the fountain of my hope
> and in whose mercy I may trust,
> than it is to long with heart and soul,
> or grow impatient, to be gone.

My spirit with His spirit groans:
Amen, Lord Jesus, quickly come!

May God bless you and keep you as you travel the remainder of your life's journey.